Are You There, God?

It's Me.
Kevin.

Are You There, God?

It's Me.
Kevin.

A Memoir

Kevin Keck

BLOOMSBURY

Map on page 76 by Dave Rohr.

Lyrics from "Two-Headed Boy, Pt. 2," by Neutral Milk Hotel,
reprinted by permission of Jeff Mangum.

A portion of chapter 7 appeared in a highly edited form on
Nerve.com. A small portion of chapter 9 appeared in a very
different form on Largeheartedboy.com.

Published by Bloomsbury USA, New York
Distributed to the trade by Macmillan

All papers used by Bloomsbury USA are natural, recyclable prod-
ucts made from wood grown in well-managed forests. The manu-
facturing processes conform to the environmental regulations of
the country of origin.

LIBRARY OF CONGRESS CATALOGING-IN-PUBLICATION DATA

Keck, Kevin.
    Are you there, God? : it's me. Kevin. : a memoir / Kevin Keck.—
1st U.S. ed.
        p.   cm.
    ISBN-13: 978-1-59691-416-2
    ISBN-10: 1-59691-416-5
    1. Keck, Kevin.   2. Conduct of life.   3. North Carolina—
Biography.   4. Syracuse (N.Y.)—Biography.   I. Title.

    CT275.K3975A3 2008
    170—dc22   2007033741

First U.S. Edition 2008

10 9 8 7 6 5 4 3 2 1

Typeset by Westchester Book Group
Printed in the United States of America by Quebecor World Fairfield

To Patrice

Her children rise up and call her blessed;
her husband also, and he praises her:
"Many women have done excellently, but you surpass them all."

—*Proverbs*

Decalogue

Fantastic doctrines (like Christianity or Islam or Marxism) require unanimity of belief. One dissenter casts doubt on the creed of millions. Thus the fear and the hate; thus the torture chamber, the iron stake, the gallows, the labor camp, the psychiatric ward.

—*Edward Abbey*

And when we break we'll wait for our miracle
God is a place where some holy spectacle lies
And when we break we'll wait for our miracle
God is a place you will wait for the rest of your life

—*Neutral Milk Hotel, "Two-Headed Boy, Pt. 2"*

A Note to the Reader

The events in this book bear resemblance to my life; thus, the characters and occurrences are quite real. However, in the interest of protecting the privacy of various individuals I have changed the names of those involved. In the matters of such artistic liberty the reader may rest assured that I have drawn freely from reality. I ask then that I not be judged as a writer given to whimsical tale-spinning, but as one possessed to record the hard truth for my neighbors, and to hope they stay awake for it.

The Revelation to Kevin

New Year's Eve 1999. It was three in the morning, and I was parked at a gas station in Scranton, Pennsylvania, checking my temperature with a rectal thermometer. I was concerned about a fever because I'd had a wisdom tooth extracted the day before, and I was paranoid about an infection. I was so paranoid that I'd been stopping every hour or so to closely monitor my vital signs. The drive from my parents' house in North Carolina to my apartment in Syracuse was an excruciating twelve hours, with ten of those hours spent on a depressing and sparsely populated stretch of I-81. My frequent stops had pushed my drive time toward the fifteenth-hour mark and I was still two hours from where I needed to be.

It had not been my plan to return to Syracuse for the New Year, but my girlfriend at the time, April, had a complete meltdown when I told her I was thinking of welcoming the Millennium in my parents' basement some seven hundred miles away from her.

"How could you fucking do this to me?" She was alternating between sobbing and yelling. "You are such a fucking bastard if you aren't here to kiss me at midnight! I fucking hate you!" She was a practicing Buddhist; we'd been dating for almost a month.

I'd been longing for a woman for quite a while—or at least a relationship that didn't smoke and melt away as quickly as a witch doused with water. The relationships I'd briefly been in over the past few years collapsed because my increasingly erratic behavior tended to exert its gravity on those people who were in my immediate orbit. The hourly thermal rectal readings I was taking as the twentieth century wound down were the least of my problems; that bit of weirdness was confined to my solitary drive. Door-knobs, polite handshakes, sick people, an obsessive fear of being stricken with food poisoning at any moment—these were the daily labors of my unquiet mind. My efforts amounted to frequent hand washings and a stern avoidance of any place I deemed dirty, and that was nearly everywhere I went. The visit to my parents' home aside, my world was confined to my apartment, the apartments of a few friends, a coffee shop, and the two eating establishments in Syracuse that passed my standards of cleanliness and palatability. I was propped up in those days by the generosity of a federal student loan system that doled out money to anyone with a pulse who could prove he or she was enrolled in college. One needn't attend classes to receive three large checks a year—I'd long ago finished my course work and I simply had to type my thesis (titled "Some Poems Mostly About Getting Laid"—it was meant to be ironic; if you have the time to write a book of poems, you aren't getting laid with any frequency) in the proper format with two-inch margins and submit it to my adviser in order to graduate. But this seemed like such a tedious process to me, and so I was in a strange purgatory with the university—it was assumed I was working on my thesis because I had not yet submitted it, thus I was enrolled in a phantom class for people in my situation that kept me technically full-time, though I in fact did nothing. I collected checks that allowed me to live a semi-lavish life (plenty of beer, plenty of dinners out, but little else) and spent the rest of my time worrying what horrific pestilence was about to be visited upon me.

When did I become so fucked up? I seem to recall thinking that as I waited for the digital thermometer to signal that it had determined the temperature in my ass—this may have been in Scranton, or possibly during any of the other dozen or so stops I'd made prior to that one, maybe even all of them. I knew it was positively insane to be worried about an infection resulting from an extracted tooth. People were not dropping dead daily from their dental procedures. Furthermore, even if I was *that worried* about an infection, why not just take my temperature as a sane man might?

I'm not entirely sure I was sane. As I was fearful of a mortal infection from a simple dental procedure—a procedure so simple that it took the dentist longer to wash his hands than to extract the tooth—it naturally follows that germs and illness freaked me out in general. (Also, I had complicated matters somewhat by passing out when injected with the Novocain . . . my mind slipped into a wonderful dream where I paddled a canoe slowly through a lush swamp with the ripples of unseen amphibians following my drift under webs of moss, and then I was disoriented and confused while the vaguely familiar woman lay a cool rag across my forehead and my dentist, Dr. Card, of whom I'd been a patient for over twenty years, with his back to me said that it was quite common for people—usually women but occasionally men—to feel woozy after an injection; I appreciated his polite way of letting me know I was a pussy.) It never entered my mind to use an oral thermometer—I'd have to be touching strange gas pumps along my route from North Carolina to New York, handling money, grasping door handles (and God forbid—door handles in *public restrooms*!), and possibly shaking hands with friendly strangers I encountered. To then use those same hands to touch a device that I would put in my mouth? The risks were too great. It was flu season. I would have to humble myself.

The use of the thermometer involved a complicated sterilization and cleanup procedure that had littered the floorboard of my 1987 Crown Victoria with rubber gloves, moist towelettes, and tissues. Were I to be pulled over for speeding, the highway patrol might have some pointed questions to ask: *Are you a sex offender? Are you a serial killer? Are you some kind of fucking nut job?*

I could put the thermometer in my mouth, keep it simple. But what about the gaping wound in my jaw? I'd heard of people getting infections after a dental procedure, and the infection eventually spread to their brain and killed them. But it was an agonizing, suffering death. Convulsions, fevers . . . fuck that. It might be extreme to plunder one's plumbing again and again with a tiny heat-sensing device, but at least I would be prepared for alien abduction.

(And in many ways I prayed for some extraterrestrials to sweep down from the heavens that night and whisk me into the timeless regions of the universe where the movement of objects slowed so much that everything appeared to be waiting . . .)

Of course, the whole drive to Syracuse I'd been snacking away on crackers and Coke, not brushing my teeth or using mouthwash—who knows what germs were running amok due to that detrimental diet? But I wasn't worried about the obvious; I'd become obsessed with the ridiculous, the improbable—I needed to be in tune with every minor nuance of the world, because if I wasn't paying attention, then I might miss a sign, some cipher that when finally decoded was a message of importance, which is to say *my importance*. The cosmos had to be paying attention to me. I meant something, and I needed to know what it was.

This tooth had put me on a collision course with the message. Nothing had made sense for a while, and I figured it was just a matter of scrutinizing my situation a little more closely. In retrospect I realize that for various reasons it was just another extension of the anxiety I'd felt since I was very young. When I was nine, I constantly worried that something dreadful was about to happen. I dreamed of my funeral; I considered the varieties of death I'd already heard of—the boy I'd gone to school with who forgot to look both ways when crossing the street, the girl who lost all her hair and then disappeared, and the two boys who just disappeared without reason, and when they did at last find them, it was in bits and pieces. These things were real and arbitrary. On the edge of sleep I would imagine everyone with a number printed on his or her wrist that only I could see, all in a march toward death. I would stay awake hoping to learn just what my number was . . .

I got over it then, but it had returned, and now I was at my wit's end with it. That final fucking year of the twentieth century was a real killer for me. Everyone was betting on the end, THE BIG FINISH—our infrastructure was a fine frog hair away from the Rapture because some dick had decided that computers should read dates as two digits instead of four.

I was on the fence about Armageddon, but if it had to go down, I preferred the whimper to the bang. Massive computer failure seemed just that: the light puff of someone sighing for the last time. At least I knew my rectal thermometer was off the grid.

However, at my stop in Scranton to verify that I was not feverish, my thermometer was not functioning as it should. I retrieved the thermometer from my ass with my latex-gloved left hand and tilted it so that I could see its readout in the glow from the streetlight adjacent to the car. It didn't display anything. I pressed the reset button and slipped the thermometer back in my ass, then peeled off the latex glove and placed it on the rear passenger-side floorboard. I then used some antibacterial hand sanitizer, then wiped my hands on a moist towelette, then wiped off the bottle of hand sanitizer with the towelette, then used the hand sanitizer again. I then wiped everything off with a tissue and waited in the pink hue of the interior: the windows were completely fogged over, and the streetlights created an eerie effect in the car.

Since midnight I'd been listening to the BBC's World Service on the radio. It was still just over twenty hours before I was swept unwillingly along into another vault of history. I hadn't yet pieced together everything that had happened the previous decade—the weight of a new century was crushing.

A reporter on the BBC interrupted whoever was reading the news to inform listeners that Boris Yeltsin, Russia's president, had resigned and handed over the nuclear codes to Vladimir Putin, a former KGB agent.

O sweet Lord, this is it. I was wrong about the business of the world's whimper—it was going out with a bang after all. The timing of everything seemed too fated, and I knew it would be half an hour or less before the rockets came raining down upon me, and I would face the apocalypse not in the arms of someone dear, but in the backseat of my shitty car, doggy-style, raping myself with a goddamned thermometer. I cursed my tooth.

The tooth was to blame because it'd been going bad for a while. A year and a half to be exact. I'd cracked it eighteen months prior on a barbecue-flavored Frito-Lay corn chip while playing pool. At the time I mistook the pain and crunch of my molar to be something from one of the corn chips. While nervously moving my tongue along my teeth a week later, I realized that half of the tooth was gone. I thought if I became diligent about brushing I could stop further decay, but my efforts were (of course) for naught. The tooth had been fine for all that time, so why did it have to send me to the dentist on the edge of the end of the world and strand me in the last place I'd ever want to be caught dead, Scranton, Pennsylvania?

The tooth had gone bad because I'd been eating too many cookies in bed and falling asleep without brushing my teeth, and I was only eating cookies in bed because I was depressed at the time about Rebecca, a lovely red-haired

Jewish queen with a perpetually runny nose and hips that
sang every sweet summer guitar solo with their sway. So,
Rebecca was to blame really, and not the tooth. But I never
would have met Rebecca had I not moved to Syracuse, and I
only moved to Syracuse because I wanted to do something
more grand with my life than any of my blood relatives had
dreamed possible with their own, and so it was my dream
that was to blame.

Yet somehow I'd lost that dream. I was less certain of
anything than I ever was before, and at that precise moment in Scranton the only thing about which I felt absolute
certainty was my impending death.

The thermometer chirped that it was ready just a split
second before the rapping on the window of my car startled
me so much that I clenched my buttocks in such a manner
as to project the thermometer out of my rectum like a failed
rocket launch: its trajectory placed it haphazardly on the
floorboard amidst the contaminated gloves and wipes.

I began to hurriedly wiggle back into my pants properly
and button them up as the tapping continued. I felt someone tug on the handle of my locked car door.

"Hang on!" I said.

"Police. Unlock the door and open it slowly."

I cast a glance at the floorboard; this could not possibly
go well.

My hands were shaking. Buckling my belt was a fruit-
less endeavor. The officer commanded me again to open
the door, though this time his voice sounded fearful and
agitated. I finally managed to buckle my belt and then
open the door—the frozen air came rushing into the car as
did a wave of nausea.

"Let me see your hands." I stuck my hands out of the car; I'd slipped a clean latex glove on my left hand while waiting for the thermometer (which I could still hear chiming on the floorboard), and I'd failed to think anything of it before opening the door.

"Okay. Out of the car." The cop had not drawn his gun, but his hand rested on his holster; he waved me toward his car and put me in the back, delicately slipping my wallet from my back pocket as he did so. I watched as he returned to my car, put his head in the backseat, then peered in the front, then the glove box and finally the trunk. He walked back over to the squad car and sat in the front. He didn't turn around and face me, but I could see his eyes in the rearview mirror.

"You sick or something?"

"I had a wisdom tooth taken out yesterday morning."

"Seriously." His eyes narrowed in the mirror.

"No, seriously. I'm just . . . You know. I worry a lot."

"Are you high?"

"No."

"Seriously." Again with the narrow eyes.

"Seriously. I'm just high-strung."

The cop laughed a little, then picked up his radio.

I listened as he called in my license. My rectum itched. I needed a moist towelette. I didn't feel fresh. I couldn't stand sitting in the back of the police car. People had probably thrown up in the back of this car, or bled, or possibly even shat themselves. I could feel my heart in my throat.

"My world is cold and without hope."

"What?" I said.

"I was reading your bumper sticker: 'My world is cold and without hope.' I hear that."

"Yeah?"

"Oh, yeah. What is it that you do?"

"I'm a student."

"See, now that's smart. I should've stayed in school, but I got married young, then the wife and I moved down here from Toronto because the money was supposed to be better. But it's not. The hours suck. So she left. Took the kid."

"That sucks."

"Screw it. What do you do? Maybe I should have stayed in school."

"Well . . ."

"I'll tell you what I should've done. I should've been a fucking fireman. Everybody loves firemen. No one loves cops. No one has ever been glad to see me unless he was about to get the shit kicked out of him, and even then . . . Well, I should've been a fireman, that's for sure."

What was I supposed to say? For all I knew, bombs from Russia were about to vaporize us all, and hell of hells, I was going to die in the back of a filthy cop car. I was probably being exposed to gonorrhea at that precise moment! And I hadn't even been able to look at the thermometer. Was I running a fever, or was the squad car merely warm? It didn't matter. I couldn't touch the thermometer—not after this. I didn't have enough hand sanitizer to put my mind at ease.

"This job . . . It's a thankless fucking job. You know what I'm saying?"

His eyes flamed at me with the green glow of his dashboard lights.

"I'm sure it's tough."

"Tough? I wish it were just tough. It's thankless. It never ends. At least your mailman gets Sundays and a few holidays."

Fantastic, I thought. *Just my luck to end up locked in the back of the police car that belongs to the world's most depressed law enforcement official.* This was all because of a tooth, which was really because of a girl, and depression, and a dream I once had that I could no longer remember.

The radio squawked that I was clear, and the cop got out of the car and opened the door for me. He handed my wallet back and stuck out his hand:

"Happy New Year, Mr. Keck."

I stared at his outstretched hand. I considered not shaking it, because who knows where a cop's hands have been? But after the exposure to his backseat I thought it couldn't hurt. I shook his hand, got into my car, and spent twenty minutes or so wiping myself down with space-age polymers designed to keep me healthy and wise. It appeared as though the bombs were going to remain in their cozy silos, and so I drove on to Syracuse with a few less worries on my mind.

The New Year's Eve party that had been shrouded in anxiety for me was long forgotten; the semester was now nearly over, and my best friends in Syracuse, Milo and J. R., had convened a whopper of a throw down at their apartment on Livingston Avenue. People didn't leave the party; they were conquered by it, and as the dawn approached, those of us who were still awake were gathered around a table in a small alcove at the back of the apartment, listening intently to a story Charlie, a professor of theology at the university, was telling about the one time he and his former wife experimented with LSD.

"It was terrible," he growled, his voice soaked in whiskey and smoke. "She was banging her head on the floor, and nothing I said would console her. So I called up a friend of ours on the phone and I said, 'Bill, the wife and I have taken some LSD. I'm completely fine, but she's banging her head on the floor and I'm afraid she's going to hurt herself. Would you mind terribly coming over to arbitrate things?'" Charlie smiled as he brought his cigarette to his mouth, but it was just an inch of ash attached to the filter; it had burned down completely during his story. He laughed at this and lit another.

"Charlie," Milo said. "You know we thought Keck was headed for the nuthatch recently."

Charlie turned as he shook the match with which he'd lit his cigarette, speaking and sending puffs of smoke across the table.

"Is that so?"

"Well, sort of . . . there was a trip to the hospital, a psychiatrist . . . nothing too serious," I said.

"They took you in an ambulance, Keck," Milo said.

"Nothing wrong with a little therapy. It happens to everyone." Charlie looked toward the window at the end of the alcove and raised his whiskey to his lips. He seemed to drift away from the conversation for a moment, and then he was back. "Sometimes you hit a rough patch. Sometimes you need a little help finding your way back."

It felt more like a sinkhole than a rough patch. I'd gone

so bonkers with my futile worries that I wound up in the hospital, dehydrated and malnourished. I was desperate for a rope to help me crawl out of this hole in my head, and so I started taking Luvox and seeing a shrink. I didn't have many sessions with the psychiatrist—his insight was to the point.

A month ago I was sitting in his office on the south side of Syracuse, the room devoid of any furnishings or decorations save for the two chairs we were sitting in and a stack of boxes in the corner.

"So, how is your work coming?" the doctor asked.

"What work?"

He pursed his lips. "Aren't you a writer?"

"Well . . ." I drifted off. "I really haven't written anything lately."

He made a note on his pad of paper. "Where did you grow up?"

"In North Carolina."

"Ah. The Bible Belt." He chuckled slightly. "Tell me, were you raised in a religious fashion?"

I considered this. I'd grown up going to church, but I wouldn't say that my family had ever been particularly religious. "Well, I went to church as a kid . . . but I really haven't been since I was an undergrad."

The doctor stroked his chin and smiled. "Good. Maybe this will be easy for you to grasp."

"What?"

"All religion is exactly what has happened to you: your obsessions and compulsions. The mind wants order. The world is confusing. Terrible things happen without reason; the wicked are rewarded. Why is this? Naturally, there is no answer, but we need an answer. Think about your time in church—what was it? It was ritual designed to give you comfort. Bad things are happening all around, people are getting sick, people need money, people need love, and these things worry us to death. And death . . . Well, that's a considerable worry for everyone. How then to alleviate these worries? You are obsessed with the disorder of the world, and so you go to this place with other people and you perform the same ritualistic behavior from week to week—occasionally there are more involved rituals, but what are those? You eat the blood and the body of Christ, you are baptized . . . How is this different than washing your hands several times a day? In both instances you are repeating a pattern that is designed to keep you safe from harm. Religion is the antidote to madness, but it is a benign madness all its own. Of course, if you aren't religious, you need to find some way to sublimate your anxieties. Some people have children, or work. You have no outlet for your obsessions, and so your compulsions have gotten away from you. Do you see what I'm saying?"

It sounded as though he was saying that there is no God, we're all fucked, and I'd best find a hobby to take my mind off the absolute terror of existence.

But that thought was only with me momentarily. The pills not only limited my leaps of logic but also my tendency toward extreme anxiety.

"Yeah, I think I get it."

"Look, I'm not saying go to church, find God, all that nonsense. This isn't a problem for a lot of people because they've never thought much about it. But if your mind is disposed toward a certain . . . introspection . . . you're going to have to find a way to redirect your mind. If it's looking for patterns in the world, it's going to go around and around until it latches onto something, and if you don't give it something, it's going to drive you mad."

I stared out the window of his office, which overlooked a series of abandoned warehouses along what was once the Erie Canal; the sky was clear, and the snow was speckled with black along the sides of the streets where it had gathered the soot from the cars shuffling back and forth.

"I think I've already gone mad," I said.

"Ha!" The doctor slapped his knee. I'd never known anyone to actually do that when they laughed. "The mad never know they're mad. You've just lost your way."

At least on that point he was right: I was positively lost. I'd wandered so far into my own head that I was having trouble finding my way back out.

I wanted to tell all of this to Charlie, but I didn't feel like rehashing the story in front of everyone else. So I said:

"Have you had any rough patches, Charlie?"

"Me?" Charlie smiled a thin, sad smile. "All the time."

"Did you see a shrink?"

"No, no. Well, from time to time. But . . ." He trailed off.

"Tell him about the cow," Milo said.

"I don't know . . ."

"Come on, Charlie," J. R. said. "I've only heard this in bits and pieces."

Charlie took a sip from his whiskey and smoked and stared out the window while we all waited. Then he said:

"Well, this was a while ago. My marriage was falling

apart; my wife had taken up with one of my students. You know, all that crap, and I'd been thinking for a few days that maybe the best option was suicide. After all, it's always an option, isn't it? So I went out for a drive through the country. I don't know why, I just felt like driving. And at some point I came to a fork in the road—a literal fork in the road where it split and went around this cow pasture. So I pulled the car over and walked to the fence that ran along the edge of the pasture. There was a cow standing by the fence, and I just stood there staring at this cow, looking into its eyes. And the cow just stood there staring at me. And then the cow asked me if I'd ever been to Guatemala."

Charlie paused to light another cigarette; I could hear everyone in the alcove breathing, the human noise, the slight shuffle of feet beneath the table.

"I had to admit that I hadn't been to Guatemala. So I went home, I took my gun from the drawer in my office, and I went into the bathroom and sat on the floor and put the gun in my mouth. And I thought about what I was doing, and everything that was a disaster, and I had my finger on the trigger.

"But that cow came into my head, and I thought, 'What is that cow doing? It's not doing anything—it's just being a cow. A cow is just a cow. It doesn't know it's a cow, it's not concerned with being a cow, and you've got to be a cow, motherfucker, you've got to do what a cow does.' I thought about that cow's eyes—it was just being a cow. And here I am, and I've never been to Guatemala, and I never will." He brought the cigarette to his mouth with the flourish of someone whose soul was truly the soul of a poet. I'd been wasting my time for the past few years in classes filled with poseurs who played the poet's part in every conceivable ridiculous manner, and yet none of them had ever said anything that seemed as real and true as what Charlie was saying. I was lost on one point, however.

"So, what exactly does a cow do, Charlie?" I asked.

"What does a cow do?" His voice rose. "Why it's just a cow, Kevin my boy. It's just a goddamned cow, and that's what you've got to do. You've got to be a cow, mother-fucker!"

Gradually, the silence around the table began to fall apart into fits of amused laughter, and when it had settled down, I said:

"Well, okay, but I'm not sure how that solves my problems."

Charlie pointed his cigarette at me and his eyes seemed to sparkle a little with the anticipation of what he was about to say: "Do you know what your problem is?"

"What?"

"You don't have any problems, motherfucker."

I left my car parked on the street in front of Milo's and I began to walk the seven or eight blocks home to my apartment. I could easily have driven; I wasn't that drunk, and Syracuse was a town designed for drunk driving: every fifty yards there seemed to be a stop sign, and if you couldn't keep your car straight for that distance, then you deserved what you got. I rarely heard of anyone getting anything as far as that goes.

But it wasn't too cold that night, and I was in one of those moods that often has a person walking the neighborhood at

an hour when most sensible people have retired for the
night. Charlie's words had shaken me yet again, and I
needed to clear my head and assess some details of my life.
Be a cow, motherfucker. I had no idea what he meant by
that. Everyone else sitting at the table had some knowing
look of the mystical third eye—my third eye was hunkered
down in my pants keeping warm, and I didn't feel this was
a situation to which he might lend his singular insight.

Did I have problems? Charlie didn't seem to think I did,
and I respected his opinion. But what the fuck? I'd grown
so obsessive about germs and all the accoutrements that go
along with that kind of psychotic thinking that I'd landed
myself in the hospital. I had no clear idea where I was
headed or what I was supposed to do with my life. For so
long I'd hung it all on this undying dream of fame, but I
lacked the talent that people seemed to care about these
days. I wrote poems. At one time I'd wanted to be a musi-
cian, but the few times I'd whipped out my guitar at
a party and launched into a sincere Pink Floyd–esque
acoustic dirge, I ended up with a lot of requests for Poison's "Every Rose Has Its Thorn," which I could never ful-
fill. Also, I couldn't sing. So I quit writing with rhymes,
and then the poems just showed up. I suppose I was pretty
good at it, but compared to the competition in the town
where I was from (we had but a single stoplight), it was
easy to stand out. It was even easy to excel at writing in
undergrad—most people had figured out by then that the
real juice was in business or marketing or sports manage-
ment. I'd always been slow on the take, and now a new
century was beginning and I didn't know what I was supposed to be doing. This wasn't a problem a few years ago,

because I still had those few years to sort it all out, but the game was afoot and I hadn't even exited the gate.

I had no logical explanation for why I was still in Syracuse. I should have been out of this place years ago. I was here simply because there was no place else I was expected. I was here out of habit. Once I was home, I fell into a heavy sleep, and the next morning I got up early and sat down in front of my computer and opened the file containing my thesis. It took me all of fifteen minutes to format it properly and print out the two copies required for submission to my adviser and the graduate school. When my roommate came home from work later that night, I told him I was moving below the Mason-Dixon Line as of mid-May; my blood was too thin for that Yankee climate.

Carolinians

By a stroke of blind luck, before leaving Syracuse, I'd managed to secure a job as a one-year faculty replacement at a private Baptist-affiliated college in the backwoods of North Carolina. The job didn't kick in until August, and so I had the summer to kill. I planned to spend it lounging around my parents' house. I had it in my head that I needed to reconnect with my roots if I was going to be able to pull it together enough to teach in the fall. Naturally my parents were more than happy to have me safely back in their orbit. I was still taking the brain pills, and as a way of relaxing further, I'd become reacquainted with the wonders of heavy pot smoking. I didn't feel I was totally out of the woods, but little by little I was shedding the anxieties that had riddled me for the previous few years.

It had only been six months since my last visit to North Carolina, but what I returned to did not at all resemble the home I remembered.

The uninterrupted forests that fanned out around the town were being cleared to make way for widened highways, new housing developments, strip malls, gas stations, and mini-warehouses—the latter being the most heinous aspect of this "progress." It was bad enough that the land that had remained largely unscathed for several hundred years was being resculpted to allow for yet another golf course lined with innumerable identical McMansions; but apparently six thousand square feet of living space could not contain all the trinkets for the bankers that commuted into Charlotte during the week. Instead they needed row upon row of flimsy aluminum storage sheds to hold their additional golf clubs, and the lamps that no longer matched the furniture, and the trunks of old photos from a time they no longer cared to remember.

Even the landscape around my parents' house had drastically changed: while I was gone, my grandparents had built a house on the acre immediately adjacent to my folks'. As it turned out, highways were being widened everywhere, and one of those projects demanded that my grandparents abandon the house they'd shared for sixty years. They received a tidy sum for their troubles—more than they would have gotten had they tried to sell the house on the open market—and so my grandfather decided to build a new home close to his oldest son, my father.

My old bedroom had long since become a storage room for the surplus of underused exercise machines that my mother invariably purchased during her manic phases of dieting, and also the excess fabric and yarn from her manic phases of crafting. (In each of the corners of my old room stood a faceless cloth doll with its blank visage turned to the wall, its hands raised to its head—leftovers from when my mother was going through a phase of making dolls with the name Punished Polly.) Thus, I was relegated to the spare bedroom, which is actually a twin bed pushed into the corner of the laundry room in the windowless basement. (The sounds of a washer and dryer still make me drowsy.)

On my first night back my mother cooked a large meal for me, my father and brother, and my dad's parents. She'd gone to a great deal of trouble preparing a roast, biscuits, gravy, mashed potatoes, black-eyed peas that had been seasoned with fatback, and collard greens simmered with a ham hock that had filled the house with the distinct smell of pork. I was still a vegetarian. I'd been a vegetarian for the last several years. My mother knew this fact quite well. My plate of mashed potatoes and a biscuit sat before me sullenly as my father said grace.

"Dear Lord, we thank you for allowing us all to be here together today. It's been a long time since we've sat down as a family, and we are indeed grateful. We thank you for bringing Kevin home to us once again"—my mom began to sniff; I raised my head and looked at her: she had her eyes closed, her face screwed up in a hideous attempt to retain her composure; my brother was glaring at me with absolute contempt—"and we are also grateful that Clyde and Margaret can share this meal with us and be close to us. We ask that you bless this food to the nourishment of our bodies. Amen."

We each affirmed our *Amen* in unison—all except for my brother, who always seemed embarrassed by group prayer.

"So, Kevin," my grandfather began, "back for good?"

I raked my fork through my mashed potatoes. "I don't know. At least for the year. It all depends on what comes up."

"Of course he's back for good," my mom said. "I've got all my babies back in the nest again."

My grandfather ignored my mother. "Well, if you find you want to stay, then stay. But if you got to go somewhere else for money, then go."

"He should go," my brother said, his mouth full of roast. Everyone ate in silence for a moment.

"Well, Kevin," my grandmother began. "Where are you living now?"

I looked at my dad; he was eyeing his plate. My grandfather was doing the same.

"Uh, I'm living here right now."

"Well, nobody told me. When did you get back?"

"Mom"—my grandfather had always called my grandmother *Mom* for as long as I could remember—"we were just talking about Kevin moving back."

"Were we? I just don't know where my mind is." She chuckled.

For at least the last year or two my grandmother had begun to repeat questions with greater frequency or get completely hung up on one topic, discussing it over and over as though she couldn't quite get the details right. Nobody thought too much about it; she was in her early eighties. If anything, she was more than entitled to be a little forgetful.

"So, Kevin," my brother said, and by his tone I could tell he was about to push one of my buttons.

My brother and I are six and a half years apart, and we've never exactly been on the same page in terms of our interests in life. Plus, I'm the first to admit that I was an absolute dick to him while we were growing up. Because I've always been small and essentially a pussy, I spent a great deal of time during my years in junior high and high school getting the shit kicked out of me in one way or another. Often these beatings were prompted by the fact that I had the absolute audacity to *read for pleasure* while riding the school bus. Because I grew up in a rural area, the school bus routes were long, meandering affairs that often took two hours to complete. By some terrible cosmic lottery I've always had the privilege of being the last stop on the bus route, and thus there were any number of sexually repressed farm boys, overly stimulated headbangers, and angry black kids all too eager to grill me about the way I chose to spend my time on the rickety ride. My inability to adequately defend myself on the bus ultimately spilled over into a rage that I took out on my younger brother, who was just as powerless against me as I was against my tormentors.

Our last altercation was as recent as the previous Christmas when I began to mock him for his collection of *Star Wars* action figures. And I'm honestly the last person to give anyone a hard time about his choice in toys. When I was twelve, I had several legions of G.I. Joe figures and enough *Star Wars* characters so that I could stage elaborate intergalactic battles. I would spend hours arranging my forces in the woods along the back of our property, or in the open field that split the space between the house and forest, and after I'd carefully placed each figure, I would take turns launching a Ping-Pong ball or tennis ball from either side, a volley of cannonballs the size of boulders to determine who would be victorious as I reigned as some tiny god over my personal Peloponnesian Wars. As I advanced toward earning my driver's license, these battles grew bloody, with more soldiers and rebel forces falling prey to the deadly pop and crack of Black Cats and M-80s. Eventually I doused an entire platoon in gasoline and watched as they melted in a napalm horror. But I became a vengeful god and boldly dashed more gasoline onto the flaming hovercraft and its perishing crew: I dropped the gas can as the fire raced up the stream of liquid toward the can, and I made it at least fifteen feet before I heard it burst in a tiny clap of thunder. After that I confined my destructive urges to my penis, and I can't say that I have too many complaints about that decision.

But my brother had just turned twenty when I was home last, and nearly every inch of two of his bedroom walls was decorated with *Star Wars* action figures, still sealed in their original packaging. I might have let that escape my ridicule—after all, I was concerned with how clean my mother kept the kitchen while I was visiting. But in addition to the figures that were displayed on his wall like some bizarre trophies of capitalistic obsession, he had duplicates of those figures displayed on shelves on the other side of his room along with the various spaceships, action-scene play sets, and other miscellaneous toys. His wall was also adorned with a Confederate battle flag and various samurai swords, nunchakus, collector-edition NASCAR pocketknives, and an Alice Cooper poster. Naturally it was only a few days before I had to say something.

"So, Brandon," I said as we were both rummaging through the kitchen pantry late one night, "it must be tough."

"What's that?"

"You know," I said, shaking a Twinkie from the box, "living with the folks . . ."

"It's not so bad. I don't have to pay rent."

". . . and having all those eyes from those *Star Wars* figures staring at you while you have sex. And when I say 'have sex,' I mean 'jack off' because there's no way you're getting laid within your shrine to George Lucas."

"Fuck you. At least Mom hasn't caught me whacking it to the computer like she did you . . . just yesterday."

"I wasn't whacking it, fuck-o. I was scratching my balls. It was dark in there. You know how Mom is." In truth I had been whacking it, but I wasn't going to own up to that. It was one thing to be caught masturbating at the age of fourteen; it was altogether another matter when you were twenty-six and attending graduate school. Such a discovery really had a way of calling into question one's intelligence.

"Yeah, whatever," my brother said, and walked off.

It went on like this for another day, each of us exchanging quips whenever the opportunity presented itself, and my brother and I had played this little game for so long that we each knew how to create an opportunity out of nothing. More than once my dad had yelled from behind the bathroom door for my brother and me to shut up—we were distracting him.

Things finally came to a head the night before I left to return to Syracuse for the New Year. I was already irritated by my bad wisdom tooth—it had started to ache the day before, and I'd managed to get an appointment for the morning of the thirtieth to have it extracted. The anticipation of having a piece of me yanked out of my head had left me on edge.

For reasons I can't exactly remember—although I'm pretty sure it was just to piss me off—my brother placed a parental block on the computer, thus preventing me from looking at porn. I asked him to fix it, he refused, and I pounced on him, pinning him down on his bed and mashing his face into the mattress as I pounded his shoulder with my fist. Because I was subsisting on a diet of PowerBars and bagels while visiting my carnivorous family, and also because my brother had gotten a great deal stronger due to his job at the factory where he helped manufacture replacement parts for antique cars, he wrenched himself free of my grip, rolled off his bed, and bounced to his feet wielding a sword he had hidden under his mattress.

"That's it," he said, and he swung at me with the sword still in its sheath. I took a shot to the ribs and went down. He unsheathed the sword. "I'm getting tired of you fucking with me."

I raised my hand in acquiescence. "Okay, okay. Understood. My bad. You win." I stood up and began to back out of the room. My brother lowered the sword and began to place it back in its sheath. That's when I grabbed the *Millennium Falcon* from where it was displayed on the shelf closest to the door and in one maneuver whipped it at his head as though I were throwing a Frisbee sidearm. My brother was faster than I gave him credit for and deflected the Falcon with the sheathed sword as though he were bunting a baseball, but it was all the distraction I needed: I dove across the room, knocking him to the ground and pressing the sword against his neck.

"So are you still tired of me fucking with—"

I felt the wind go out of me and I collapsed on top of him at about the same time he had the good sense to ferociously knee my balls. I rolled into a heap and saw my dad wielding a fireplace poker, his face red and his hands shaking. I couldn't get a breath to form any words, and that was probably quite a stroke of luck. It was my brother who started to commend my dad for coming to his rescue, but my brother's voice seemed to piss my dad off just that much more, and he reached down and yanked my brother from the ground and with a single push sent him sailing across the room, where his impact against the wall crushed the plastic that encased his sealed action figures; the grief on his face as he heard the sound of the plastic crinkling under his weight was absolutely priceless, and I would have laughed had there been oxygen in my lungs.

But I also knew it was time to make a hasty retreat; I'd witnessed my father's temper perhaps three other times in my life. He was a man possessed when he hit his boiling point, because usually he was the picture of absolute even-temperedness. He'd clearly lost all inhibitions. I didn't want to find out what else he might do with that fire poker. I managed to get a gulp of air, and I started to get to my feet. My dad grabbed my arm and yanked me up the rest of way, tightening his grip and twisting my arm.

"And if you're just going to come home and eat our food and be an asshole, why do you even bother? You fruitcake!" I couldn't figure out why my dad was accusing me of being gay, and then I realized he was taking a dig at me over the frequent hand washing he'd witnessed the past few days, and my tendency to wash an apple three times in dish detergent before I would eat it. It didn't seem right to take such a cheap shot, and I wasn't in the mood to feel powerless against my father. Even though I'd gotten into the graduate writing program at Syracuse by only submitting a writing sample (and not even an application), my dad was still not supportive of my desire to be a writer. He continually mentioned that Syracuse had a fine law school, and that a lot of lawyers were able to make a good living while practicing writing in their spare time, and if I got lucky, well, then I could afford to make my hobby my vocation. I felt a rage well within me.

I shoved him—he was surprisingly hard to budge from his footing, but he did take a step backward and it placed him with one foot insecurely upon the downed *Millennium Falcon*, and that was all it took to send him reeling into my brother's display shelves, which were fastened to the walls by a series of brackets that were not designed to withstand the thrust of someone tumbling into them. My dad collapsed to the floor amidst an avalanche of action figures and plywood.

I didn't loiter to determine if either my brother or dad was hurt—I felt someone needed to be removed from the equation, and I unanimously elected myself to that position. I fled out the back door and into the yard, not breaking stride until I'd reached the edge of the woods, where I climbed into the tree house that my brother and dad and I had built in another lifetime. I sat there feeling like a prick and agonizing over my desperate need to wash my hands. I sat on my hands with my legs dangling off the edge of the tree house, and after the lights went out in my folks' place, I entered through the basement, immediately washed my hands, and slept on the couch downstairs because no one would think to look for me there, and also because I'd hear the floor creaking above me before anyone took me by surprise in the basement. I had my tooth extracted the next morning, and shortly after that I left for Syracuse without telling even my mother good-bye.

So that was how things stood with my brother and the effect our adversity had on people within our immediate influence, which is why I cringed when he shoved his mouth full of collard greens and said in his most baiting tone, "So, Kevin . . ." I waited as he chewed and swallowed. "If you're going to use the computer, be sure to wipe the lotion off the mouse when you're done." He took a sip of his iced tea as he stifled a laugh.

Fortunately, I'd brought a substantial quantity of marijuana back from New York with me. The proximity of Syracuse to the Canadian border meant that there was always an ample supply of well-priced Canadian bud. Plus it was a college campus with a significant population of wealthy kids from Long Island—it was a given that good weed was never hard to locate. Thus, I was pleasantly stoned, and I had to admit that I found my family to be a great deal more amusing than what I remembered. I smiled at my brother. "I'll use my left hand," I said. "Mom, could you pass the biscuits?"

For the next several weeks I made a serious effort to avoid my brother, and it turned out to be easier than I thought. He left early in the mornings for his job at the factory, and by the time he came home in the afternoon I'd driven to the park where I sat on the swings and smoked pot, or I'd driven to an old friend's house where we sat around and smoked pot, or I just wandered off into the woods behind my parents' house, passing the time wondering what the names of all the plants were. After a while I just started giving them names of my own invention, such as Fred, or Victoria, or Serena. I found that this activity amused me to no end. Sometimes I would talk to the plants—not under the delusion that they would really talk back, mind you, but the frequent pot smoking was beginning to change the manner in which I was relating to the world. Before my collapse and subsequent trip to the hospital I'd felt completely apart from reality, as though I were at war with it, constantly wrestling with whether something was broken with my head or broken with the world. Because I remembered what it was like to be filled with a sense of purpose and direction, I opted for a broken head, and when I was stoned, I felt as though the leaks were being repaired. For the first time ever I was feeling *connected* to what was around me. I wasn't worried that I had no idea what I was doing with my life—everything was simply *cool*.

Of course, not everything was as kosher as I would've liked. Every so often the old thoughts tried to stage a coup: it was hard not to wash a piece of fruit with soap before eating it; I occasionally still wouldn't eat the portion of the sandwich that had touched my skin, as I was fearful some renegade germs on my hands might make me violently ill.

I didn't have too much money to spare, so I didn't leave the house as much as I would have preferred. When I'd grown weary of everything else, I'd wander down to my grandparents' house.

Their previous home had begun as a two-room affair that my grandfather paid some local fellows to build in 1938. It had a kitchen, a bedroom, and a porch. The bathroom was a good twenty-yard walk away. My grandfather had gotten the land from his father-in-law, and thus my grandmother spent eighty years of her life on the same half acre of land. By the time the house was demolished by the state, it had acquired an additional five rooms, including a bathroom and a garage, all built by my grandfather and therefore possessing the quirks of craftsmanship that are the signature of the amateur carpenter.

The new home was three thousand square feet of pre-manufactured ranch blandness. Essentially, a basement had been built, and two trucks and a crane came and placed the halves of a home conceived in a factory on top of the foundation and hammered them together as easily as LEGOs. The house smelled plastic and sterile, like an airtight box designed for scrapbooks.

In fact, it didn't seem as though anyone actually lived there. When my grandparents moved, my aunts and uncles decided to buy them new furniture, and so it appeared my grandparents were living in a display home—everything was so new my grandfather never quite looked entirely relaxed when sitting in his La-Z-Boy, as though he were afraid he might spill his drink on the fabric and have to pay for it.

I often knocked on their door shortly after lunch—I'd initially started going down before lunch because my grandmother was a tremendous cook, and she often cooked several pots of vegetables at a time, but her culinary skills had declined with her memory. When I'd first returned from Syracuse, my grandmother said that if I'd come over for dinner one afternoon (in the old Southern vernacular, *dinner* and *lunch* are interchangeable terms), she'd cook a chicken. I didn't feel like explaining to her that I was a vegetarian.

When I appeared promptly at eleven thirty the next day, their usual hour for lunch as long as I could remember, I found my grandmother in the kitchen putting slices of bologna between pieces of thinly sliced white bread. No chicken was in sight, or anything else that might accompany a chicken dinner.

"Decide not to cook a chicken, Mamaw?"

She turned around and smiled at me. "Well, honey, I've made chicken salad sandwiches."

I thought she was kidding, but something in her tone caused me not to call her on it. She walked over to the top of the stairs and called into the basement where my grandfather and dad were perpetually occupied with trying to restore the motor on a John Deere riding lawn mower from 1972. Both of them had brand-new mowers that were far superior to the one that had become an albatross of the lawn-care variety; I had no idea why they insisted on wasting their time with it.

"Clyde! David!" she yelled. "I've made chicken salad." She walked back into the kitchen and placed the bologna sandwiches on plates. "Well, grab yourself a plate and sit down. We hardly see you anymore."

"You just saw me yesterday," I said.

"I did?" My grandmother seemed genuinely puzzled. "Well, you live so far away it's hard for me to keep up."

"I live next door, Mamaw."

"When did you start living next door? Did you move back from Charlotte?"

"Mamaw, I haven't lived in Charlotte in over five years."

This seemed to agitate my grandmother. "Well, where have you been? Why doesn't anyone tell me these things?"

"I've been at school in New York."

"New York?" She spit the words out like bitter seeds. "What were you doing with all those Yankees?"

About that time my grandfather and dad came into the kitchen, both of them smudged with grease along their arms.

"Mother," Dad said, "what have we got here?"

"Just some chicken salad," she said.

My grandfather picked up his plate and looked at my dad. My grandfather was turned away from me, so I don't know what emotion passed over his face, but my dad gave me a look of *Just don't say anything* . . . I discreetly slipped the bologna from my sandwich and tossed it in the trash, then ate the two pieces of white bread as though it were the most delicious chicken salad I'd ever had in my life.

Ultimately, the slow drift of summer began to grate upon me. The chess game of avoiding my brother was wearing me out, and spending time with my grandparents was an exercise in just how much depression I could bear. It was as if the move from the family land had dislocated my grandmother somehow. Most of the time she was cognizant of the events happening around her, but every so often she seemed to slip through a rift in time, and a sentence that she spoke would betray the fact that she was no longer in the same year as we, but had instead returned to a place more vivid for her than the present surroundings.

My family was fond of playing a variation of croquet that resembled golf. After one such game in late June, my parents, grandparents, and I were sitting in the shade of the mimosa trees listening to the crickets tuning up for the evening. My brother had traveled to South Carolina for a comic book convention.

I don't recall exactly what we were talking about—possibly the upcoming election in the fall. My family is of Democratic stock, and everyone was cheerful that George W. Bush would be the likely candidate for the Republican Party. We knew there wasn't a chance that he would win because the American people were generally sensible when it came right down to it, and there was the premature speculation of how an Al Gore administration might extend the prosperity that we'd enjoyed under President Clinton. During a lull in the conversation my grandmother said:

"Well, Clyde, I suppose we'd best be getting back home before it gets too dark."

"I don't think you have too far to go," my dad said. He laughed and my grandfather smiled sadly.

"Well, David," she said, "we've got to go all the way to Hickory. That's a right long drive."

"Mom," my grandfather said, "we don't live in Hickory anymore. Our house is right here." He pointed at the house that was twenty feet or so from where we were all sitting. My grandmother looked absolutely puzzled.

"Quit fooling, Clyde. You know where we live."

My grandfather raised his glass of tea to his mouth and began to crunch up a piece of ice with his dentures.

"Margaret, you live next door to us now, remember?" My mom put her hand gently on my grandmother's knee.

"Oh, bullshit, Amanda."

I'd never once heard my grandmother curse.

"Mom," my grandfather said, "this is our house now. That house in Hickory isn't there anymore. We *are* home."

My grandmother turned her face from us and looked toward the line of trees that had grown thick with shadows as the sun settled behind them.

"Well, Clyde," she said, "I'm ready to go home when you are."

My plan for pulling myself together wasn't working out exactly as I'd imagined it. I used to be able to retreat to my parents' house, my childhood home, and find the sort of mooring that kept me from drifting further into the storm-swept waters of personal uncertainty. Now I felt as though I were being held together entirely by chemical compounds instead of the love of people who shared my blood and the continuity of a place that had remained unchanged for most of my life. It was a tremendous event when, during my sophomore year in high school, my town was finally graced with its first fast-food restaurant: Burger King. You would have thought that the mother ship had landed to extend intergalactic greetings to the bipedal creatures inhabiting the outer edges of the Milky Way—such was the impact of a mediocre chain burger joint. And now there were rumors in the local paper of Wal-Mart eyeing Denver, North Carolina, as the next possible conquest for their Alexandrian Empire of Capitalism. I hadn't gotten any closer to reconnecting with my sense of self—I felt further out in the deep waters than I had before, but at least I was sublimating. Technically, I suppose what I was doing was *medicating*, but no matter—at least I was able to face a doorknob with confidence.

Since I'd gotten back home, my mom and dad (but

mostly my mom) had been after me to start attending church with them. While I'd been away, my folks had become members of a different church from the one I'd grown up in. I wasn't clear on the particulars of this, but from what I gathered it had something to do with my mom's arrest some months back for assaulting a police officer. My mom tended to spend most of her time in her bedroom, rising only for the call of nature or the braying of snack cakes, but on occasion she had been known to rouse herself for more nefarious purposes.

While I was away in Syracuse worrying about whether I should buy the box of macaroni and cheese that looked as though it had been slightly dented during shipping, my mom was at home worrying about false accusations concerning her flatulence.

I've never been especially close to my mother's side of the family. This is mainly by my mother's own design—her family has remained in the same hollow in the Appalachian Mountains as long as anyone can remember. Her ancestors—my ancestors, too, when you get right down to it—were that independent and unruly stock of men who left their farms and families to vex Cornwallis as he tried to wrestle the southern colonies into submission on behalf of good King George. That allegiance to *their land* and no one else's is strong in the blood that has flowed down to my mother and to me.

But my mom also inherited the curse that has carried me up and down the East Coast—that dream of something larger than the little lives we were born into. As the eighth of nine children in a family where the children were more laborers than blessings, my mom had to fight to find her place. Eventually she found it in books, which may not seem so strange, but as I write, my mother's oldest brother toils in some anonymous stretch of the Blue Ridge, growing Christmas trees for the bankers and doctors and lawyers that make the pilgrimage from the cities with their families annually after Thanksgiving to select their *Tannenbaum*, and if they ever think to send him a card wishing good tidings for the season, he cannot read it. He's a brilliant carpenter and arborist, but one need not be literate to be a master craftsman.

I imagine how different our worlds are . . . Everything I know I understand through words, nuanced and malleable, each love lost fit for verse or tomb, each experience an adornment for an unknown room, a door waiting to be unlocked with language. My mother began stealing books from the library and climbing a tree in the thick of the apple orchard that extended behind the farmhouse. No one in her immediate family grasped what the books meant to her, and she caught hell for her indulgence: if it wasn't her father taking a shaving strap to her backside, then it was her younger brother and one of his friends continually chasing her and wrestling her to the ground, taking her books and handling her in a manner that she's never seemed comfortable discussing.

As I understand it, my mother began to tell the stories from the books as though they were her own. She related these tales to her schoolmates, all of whom knew she was lying. But as she remembers it, no one ever called her on her deception—they seemed as eager as she was to escape the drab existence of subsistence farming, and a future that was too familiar in the bent backs of their sharecropping parents.

My mother has told me that no one was very interested in the stories of the supernatural, but they were completely intrigued by Damon Runyon's tales, or the story of young Holden Caulfield wandering through New York City—the merciless urban jungle was their greatest nightmare. You must understand that my mother grew up in a church where one's faith was tested by the handling of snakes, and those in deep communion with God babbled in tongues at once exhilarating and frightening; Edgar Allan Poe had little to offer them in the way of escapism.

My mom was only the second person in her family to graduate from high school, and somehow she managed to maneuver her way into a college scholarship. When she arrived at college, she met my father, so I suppose it's fair to say that I was born because of a love of books.

My mother's dream took her out of the hollow, and just as if she'd ceased believing in Avalon, the mists of memory grew heavy and she could no longer find her way back into that tightly knit tribe whose DNA matched her own.

To a certain extent my mother shares some of the blame in her alienation from her family. She's managed to drop the accent that might tip people off to her place of origin, and when she arrived at college, she told anyone who asked that she didn't have a family; she was an orphan.

Humans are curious creatures, though, especially when it comes to that innate need to feel rooted to a geography or a group of people, and ultimately over the years my mom has tried to mend fences with her family. Her success has been uneven at best, often leading to more harsh words, more feuds. In her defense, while she was in intensive care recovering from a double mastectomy, none of her family ever came to visit her.

I don't know whom to believe where the fart is concerned; I don't even know what prompted it, and I'm not even sure that it matters. All I know is that in October of 1999, my cousin Wanda accused my mother of calling her at two in the morning, farting into the telephone, and hanging up.

For most people this would be a matter worthy of nothing more than a good laugh. For my mother it was a serious point of honor. I was absent for the duel of charges volleyed back and forth over a series of weeks between my mother, my cousin, and my aunts. And finally my mother reached her breaking point. She removed the tire iron from her white Lincoln Town Car, got in the driver's seat, and went to pay my cousin a visit.

This story is already a tenuous tale in terms of its reliability—I am not a witness to any of it, but rather a collector of interpretations from various parties who saw the before and after of the ordeal. Only my mother went to see my cousin, and my cousin refuses to speak to anyone about whatever occurred. This is how I understand it:

My mother, in one of her less brilliant moves, called ahead to let my cousin Wanda know that she was coming to kick her ass. This was foolish on a number of levels, not least of which is that Wanda's husband is an officer with the Department of Corrections. Granted, that position doesn't really carry the weight that it might were he actually a police officer, but it's a small town where they live, and of course all the people who enforce the laws in one way or another have a loyal bond. According to my mother, she merely pulled in Wanda's driveway, honked her horn, and when Wanda came to the door, my mother stuck her arm out her car window and extended her middle finger. Then she drove off.

According to the statement given to the police, my mother drove by the house several times waving a tire iron out the window.

My mother has no recollection of doing either. In fact, she does not even remember driving to my cousin's house. Her memory kicks in at the moment she's being arrested.

I don't know what to make of this. My dad has said that when he went to retrieve the car from the impound lot, a tire iron was lying in plain view on the passenger-side floorboard. My mother has stuck to her guns about the fact that she never had a tire iron at all.

Part of my problem with the reliability of the facts of this story goes back to the summer I was nineteen and living with my parents. My habit at that time was to sleep until noon. I don't think this is uncommon among people exiting their teenage years—those hormones are positively exhausting. Also, masturbating frantically from midnight until four in the morning requires a certain amount of recovery.

On one morning my mother woke me up with a butcher knife pressed against my throat, and she was screaming, "Goddammit! Get up, you bitch, or I'll kill you!" I got up, but I made sure she had withdrawn the blade before I bounced from the bed. After I'd dressed and pulled myself together, I went to find my mother and explain to her that she was crazy and that I was calling Dad.

I found her in the kitchen making cookies.

"Hi, sugar plum." She seemed convincingly cheerful.

"What the fuck is wrong with you?"

"I beg your pardon? Don't use language like that with your mother."

"Have you lost your mind? No, wait—don't answer that. You've clearly lost your mind because you just *held a fucking butcher knife to my throat!*"

"What?" She was looking me dead in the eye.

"What do you mean, 'What?' You know what—you just woke me up with a knife to my throat."

She wrinkled her brow and regarded me with a leery curiosity. "Are you sure you weren't dreaming?"

"Dreaming? I felt the blade against my throat."

"That must have been a vivid dream."

"Are you fucking with me? You're fucking with me. I'm calling Dad. You've lost it."

I picked up the phone and began to dial my dad's work number.

"Go ahead and call your father. I don't know what you're talking about. I've been in here baking cookies the whole time."

"Like a fucking witch in a gingerbread house."

"I said not to talk to me like that."

"Sorry, Mom—all bets are off. You pulled a knife."

When I got my father on the phone, I explained what had happened, and he let out an all-too-knowing sigh. "Put your mother on the phone."

"David," she said, "I don't know what he's talking about. I think he's just had a vivid dream . . . Mmhm . . . Okay. I'll tell him." She hung up the phone. "Your father said for you to mow the grass."

Years later I felt the need to press this issue if only to

confirm that my own memory was reliable, and she admitted that she knew exactly what I was talking about.

"Why did you lie to me?" I asked. "Don't you understand how that's fucked with my head all this time?"

"It got you up, didn't it?"

The saga of my mother's visit to Wanda's becomes as impossible to verify as JFK's assassination. *Was a fart seen on the grassy knoll? Or did it come from the book depository window?* Either way, as soon as she left Wanda's, a local cop was waiting for her at the end of the street. My mother was pulled over, asked to step from her vehicle, and she complied. But when the cop was within range, she hocked up a mighty ball of phlegm and launched it straight into his face. (I at least know that part is true, because that's what got her arrested; not the threat with the tire iron.) The cop then pepper-sprayed my mother, who would have been fifty years old at the time and hardly a physical threat, and took her downtown.

My dad left her in jail that night. I suspect he was by this point at his limit with my mother. We'd moved to Denver when I was seven, in part because my mother couldn't get along with the neighbors we had in Banner Elk. We moved from our first house in Denver because it was in a subdivision, and my mother couldn't get along with those people either. Since our second house was out in the country and completely isolated from other humans, my mom's insistence on stirring up trouble has been localized to the immediate family. To hear my dad tell it, that night my mom spent in jail was one of the finest nights of rest he'd had in quite some time.

The next morning when my father went to pick up my mom from the jail, he took their pastor with him. For my mother this was an injustice greater than the accusation of the fart—how dare she be shamed in front of her minister! Never mind that if anyone should offer her unconditional solace it should be her Lord's emissary, but it was not something she could ever get over. If one had to appear sinless before anyone, it was certainly one's minister. Thus, my parents switched their church membership.

Of course, the church they started attending was only a few miles down the road from their previous one, so it's not as if this move carried any great significance.

For me, the reality was that I lived in a very small town, and if I wanted to meet a woman, I had three choices: school, church, and the hardware/feedstore. I was too old by this point to be prowling the high school, and I've never been good with tools or animal husbandry. The alternative to church was driving the twenty-six miles into Charlotte where people actually did things, such as go to bars and drink and shout small talk at each other over the pounding of jukeboxes that seemed perpetually too loud. Trying to pick up a girl while yelling at her and still retaining some degree of coolness has never been my strong suit, and so it was clear that the church would offer a more restrained background volume, over which I could practice my most pious pickup lines.

Though the people at church were generally gregarious and not entirely unpleasant to be around, and despite my father's promise that there were "good-lookin' babes in the pews every Sunday," my luck was as dismal as ever. Besides, I forgot to factor in that my father's equation for beauty was formulated quite differently from mine: he was in his sixties and from a different era, so a fine crop

of plump, tanned, bright blonde girls were the answer to
his prayers; I preferred my women pale, dark-haired,
bone-thin, and troubled (a mild relationship with an eating disorder wasn't entirely undesirable either—those
girls are in desperate need of protein, and I know a good
source).

I drifted through weeks of well-rehearsed sermons
(which certainly didn't help my dating cause, not to mention my depression) while trying to remind myself of who I
was and where I'd come from. I realized only too late that I
was twenty-seven years old and living in my parents' laundry room, and this did little to quiet my mind about my
being a fucking loser. The days could not pass quickly
enough, and I soon found myself looking for any method to
spring me from the madness of my mother's maternal med-
dling. ("Are you eating enough, Kevin?"; "I met this nice
girl at the consignment shop, Kevin, I got her number for
you."; "Do you need Mommy to hold you, baby?") I was
ready to be abandoned in the woods—and I tried for just
exactly that, applying with the government for a position as
a fire lookout in Arizona, ready to forsake the faculty position that waited for me in an August that dangled in a too
distant future; with my master's degree in creative writing
(with a concentration in poetry) I was deemed "overquali-
fied" to look for plumes of smoke.

After the eight thirty a.m. service on Sundays there was
a "coffee hour." It was actually only half an hour, but I
suppose the church ladies on the coffee committee—
churches are nothing but a confederation of committees—
had the good sense to recognize that "coffee half hour" is
a clunky name. I only went to the early service because my

parents didn't, and also, as it was the first service of the day, a schedule had to be maintained. The minister tended to stray into improvised bits at the second service, often exceeding the hour that Methodists will tolerate for a sermon and all the trappings. Typically during football season and March Madness he kept his forays into the anecdotal deserts to a minimum, as parishioners would skip a service if they felt it would cut into pregame activities, therefore lessening the collection for the week.

Thus, I was guaranteed a short sermon by rising early, and the coffee half hour provided the most likely opportunity to scope out the hidden gems—those third-generation farmer's daughters that give the lonely hearted of small Southern enclaves something to hope for and fight over.

Hope was really the operative word. Most of the women at the church who were hovering in their late twenties as I was had already hedged their bets and were settling into lives with stable-income providers. I was temporarily in my parents' basement—I had nothing to offer, and so I often just stood up against the wall in the basement of the church in the large meeting room where the coffee half hour was held, coveting the wives and girlfriends of other men. The girls who were back home for summer from college never gave me the time of day. They must have recognized my leering, lust-starved look from the prematurely balding grad students at their own schools.

I don't know why I was getting up early on Sundays and faithfully attending services, except that I felt I needed some sort of routine, an anchoring to keep my mind from drifting off again. Serotonin boosts and herbal relaxation were only capable of doing so much, and the safety net of my family was seriously frayed. Whenever my grip on the world had slipped in the past, I'd been able to lash myself to the certainty of blood. It quickly became clear that I was going to have to navigate my way back to my old self on my own: between my mother and grandmother, my dad and grandfather had their hands full, and one more lunatic on the menu was destined to sink us all. My best friend from undergrad, Luke, still lived in Charlotte, but he had a job and responsibilities that were hard for me to fathom, and whenever we'd gotten together since my return from Syracuse, he'd dismissed my troubles as little more than the neuroses of someone with too much time on his hands. At one point I'd trusted Luke as much as anyone, and if he shared the opinions of Charlie and the psychiatrist back in Syracuse, then it must be so: I needed some business in which to immerse myself.

The whole move back to familial territory was beginning to seem like a colossal mistake. With nothing to do but sit around and count the days and catalog the television programs, I had time to reflect on what I'd left behind: steady pussy and free access to a state-of-the-art gymnasium. I could have spent forever accumulating debt and imagining a grand interdisciplinary thesis, and when I became too old to date undergrads, I'd move on to grad students and then, ultimately, faculty. If all went well, I'd suffer a coronary while humping some tenured, tanned assistant professor in the foreign languages department. Not bad for a dilettante.

A month or so of Sunday mornings passed that found me mumbling feigned greetings to church members and otherwise sulking half-asleep, half-stoned over a foam cup of the most hellishly abysmal coffee—its blandness truly captured the flavor of Southern Protestant Christianity. Those Catholic monks might seem a little nuts, but at least the weirdness caused by the absence of any real romantic relationships drives them to a level of excellence in other endeavors, particularly the production of beer. Without a monastic system the Protestant palate has lapsed into an unquestioning acceptance of total mediocrity. When I was growing up, I knew of only a few Catholic families, and nearly all of them had a certain air of sophistication that I was never quite able to identify. Now I get it: whereas a Catholic treats kitsch as ironic, a typical Bible-thumping Southern Protestant finds it *iconic*. Thus, Elvis lovingly rendered in airbrush on black velvet.

The crowd lingering for coffee thinned in July. During one of the postmortems the choir director mentioned having seen me in a local theater production of *Grease* some years ago—it still chills me that my performance has lingered in a memory outside of my own. I do not have the talent to be an actor, let alone one that sings and dances, but there was a time when I refused to let such obstacles stop me, and since I was living in an area that wasn't really known for its fine thespians, I could occasionally get a part. And that's how I ended up playing Roger, King of the Mooners, in the Lincoln Theater Guild's 1992 extravaganza of *Grease*. I probably have a great many things to be embarrassed about in my life, but this rises to the top of the list.

But the choir director had a different memory of it altogether. She recalled it as "wonderful," and I had yet to catch a glimpse of sarcasm among any of the church members.

"You know," she said, "part of our mission at the church is outreach through dramatic programs."

"That's good," I said. "I hear it's supposed to be hot to-day."

"Well, it is July. Look—do you still do any acting?"

"No, not really." I had a terrible feeling in my stomach; I sensed where this was going. I'd been caught with my emotional shields down, and my ability to retaliate with the necessary rejection was not fully charged and ready to be deployed.

"Well, we've got this program coming up in a few weeks as part of the worship service. It's just a short skit about Jesus feeding the multitudes, but we really need another man. Do you think you might be interested in helping?"

Arrgh. There it was. I'd been asked to help.

I don't mind helping people, but I like to do it when it's most convenient for me. I had absolutely no desire to help in any way with a mystery play that was to be performed in front of the church congregation, but I felt powerless to resist. I left the church that day with a copy of a three-page play and set about learning my lines. The whole matter might be embarrassing, but it wouldn't be because I didn't know my dialogue.

My grandmother was declining gradually. Bologna sandwiches were fast becoming the rule rather than the exception; everyone treated this as a minor eccentricity until my grandmother served a plate of bologna sandwiches one Saturday afternoon with the bologna placed between paper napkins instead of bread.

A week after I received my lines for the play I was at my grandparents' house, halfheartedly going over my neurotic dialogue, which had me lamenting the absence of bread and salted fish. The play was based on the sixth chapter of the Gospel of John where Jesus feeds five thousand people with five loaves of bread and two fish. If you have but a loose association with the church, then you have most likely heard this story of Jesus whipping up a thirty-minute meal.

I walked down into the basement where my dad and grandfather were standing over the lawn mower's engine, carefully studying some recently dissected parts. My dad was saying:

". . . no, I don't recall if that screw went to that piece or not."

"Well," my grandfather said, "we could just use some duct tape. It won't hurt it . . ."

I walked up beside them and looked at what they were examining.

Without looking at me my dad said, "Kevin, can you tell if this screw"—he held a small bolt between his thumb and index finger—"goes to this right here?" He tapped on a part of the lawn mower's engine with a screwdriver. I didn't even know the name of the part he was tapping on.

"No," I declared, "I don't think so."

The three of us stood silently staring at the lawn mower's exposed pieces.

"Clyde! Clyde!" my grandmother's frantic voice echoed down the stairs.

"Mom, I'm downstairs!"

We heard her slow gait on the steps, then she appeared around the corner.

"When are we going home?" she said.

My grandfather smiled sadly. "We are home, Mom. This is our home."

"Clyde, we came here on an airplane. How could this be our home?"

My dad and I looked at each other; my grandfather returned his gaze to the lawn mower.

"Mother," my dad said, "what airplane?"

"Why, it's right here in my pocket." She began to reach into the pockets of her Hawaiian-print housedress. "Well, I had it a minute ago. I guess we could just take the car."

My grandfather didn't lift his head. Without saying anything my dad slowly turned his head back to the mower.

"Come on, Mamaw. I'll walk back upstairs with you," I said.

"Well, hey, Kevin. When did you get here?"

This was one of the last occasions when my grandmother would recognize me without hesitation. It was humid and the weight of summer seemed suspended in the damp air, oppressive and clinging, and I wanted to shake it off and put as much distance between me and where I was as quickly as possible. What had I imagined was waiting for me here? More and more it appeared as though I'd come back simply because I didn't know where else to go.

My grandmother had a minor stroke that night as she slept, further fraying the fragile synapses that bridged the *then* and *now*, and limiting her mobility. In retrospect, this seems like something of a blessing: I didn't know it at the time, but my grandmother had started wandering outside without telling my grandfather where she was going. Several times he'd found her in the passenger seat of their car with her purse in her lap, waiting patiently to be taken home. At least once he'd caught her just as she was about to drift into the road—a frightening prospect as that road is a favored shortcut between two major highways, and I've lost more than a few pets to hurried commuters. The stroke kept her body from wandering, but it set her unanchored mind adrift on the currents of memory, and she became a wave forever after, rippling along the shore and perpetually receding.

Overnight she was thrust into diapers, and my grandfather was forced into something he'd managed to avoid his whole life: housework. It seems a cruel twist that one should make it into one's eighties and be suddenly obliged to learn how to cook. It made my grandfather a staunch advocate of the microwave dinner.

My own benign brush with a disconnected mind was still fresh, and so my grandmother's total departure from reality was an unpleasant reminder of what the world could serve up. I started to search for an apartment that week. When I found one, I sold my computer, put down the deposit and first month's rent, and moved in early. My family was more of an anvil than an anchor, and I had no desire to stand among them as the dark waters rose around us. I did the bit part at the church, and when the choir director asked me after the service to assist with their next dramatic production, I politely said no. I'd made the mistake once, and I wouldn't do it again. The closest I planned on getting to organized religion involved my employment at the Baptist college, but that was it. I wasn't coming back.

The Gospel of Luke

Things didn't go as planned at the Baptist college. Thus, by the spring of 2001 I was living on the couch that belonged to Luke, my roommate from my last year of undergrad. What was ironic was that I'd given him the couch when I'd left for Syracuse because without it he possessed only a single chair; such an arrangement was unthinkable, considering the circumstances of his life when I left.

Luke had taken me in during our senior year after my parents kicked me out of the house for running up a large phone-sex bill. At the time he didn't live anywhere near the campus, and so we easily became coconspirators in the business of cutting class. Instead of following a formal track of education we sat around his apartment smoking cigarettes and reading Douglas Coupland, Jack Kerouac, Charles Bukowski, and acting out the plays of Sam Shepard. It was a sweet time, and Luke's trust fund, which he cashed in shortly after my arrival, made it all that much sweeter.

However, in the six years since I'd last lived with Luke, he'd gotten his girlfriend pregnant, married her under pressure from his fanatically religious parents, and was divorced shortly after the baby was born. His ex-wife retained custody of their daughter and then married the guy that Luke had stolen her away from in the first place; and Luke had, for the last three years, driven every Wednesday up to Winston-Salem where his ex-wife lived and slept on the couch beneath her and her husband's bedroom so that he could spend time with his daughter. And he worked his ass off to pay child support. Needless to say, a slight, if unspoken, undercurrent of tension flowed between Luke and me: I'd been the one who assured him that if he cashed in his trust fund, we could play the stock market and double, *if not triple*, that money ever so easily. We never made it to the stock market, but we did make it to the liquor store on any number of occasions.

Also, it might've just been in my head, but I was nagged by the constant feeling that Luke had never quite forgiven me for leaving. We were as close as brothers, and it had come to light in the weeks before I left for Syracuse that his girlfriend was pregnant. The ties that held us were slowly unraveling because of my imminent departure, and that he was about to become a father cut them free completely. We'd managed to wander into different dreams somehow—I was going off to become a writer; Luke was going to raise a family.

Except that Luke didn't want to raise a family. He was also skulking down that elusive path of the professional artisan; he just happened to have the good fortune to date a woman who didn't mind getting fucked without a condom. I had a girlfriend at that time, too, but she wasn't stupid.

During one of the few visits I had with Luke between 1995 and 2001, he told me he'd wept uncontrollably before his nuptials, and that he had actually *prayed to God* that I was on my way to the wedding to rescue him and smuggle him out of the state.

"Can you believe that?" he said, nearly knocking his beer over where we sat at the bar. "I fucking prayed, and you know I believe there's not a bigger waste of time in the world than that. It's this God nonsense that had me in that situation in the first place. If my parents weren't so fucking up the Lord's tight imaginary asshole, they never would have laid that guilt on me so thick that I felt I had to marry Tina. I knew it was a mistake, but when they get those hooks in you early on . . . you know? It's hard to shake that fire-and-brimstone bullshit."

When I landed at Luke's for the second time in my life, I'd been living in North Carolina almost a year. Around February I'd quit taking the brain pills; their purpose seemed to have been served, and essentially they were impeding my ability to experience total sexual pleasure. (I've yet to take an antidepressant that hasn't had such a side effect.) I was content teaching composition part-time, and getting high from the instant I opened my eyes until the moment my eyes could no longer withstand the level of THC in my bloodstream. I'd rediscovered my appreciation for the Grateful Dead, Phish, fusion-era Miles Davis, and every other band with a tediously meandering sensibility, songs that digressed to the point where no one—including the musicians—seemed entirely certain where the songs started in the first place. I was learning to let go of my worries, even the worry that said, *Good God! Shouldn't this song be over by now?*

Luke was easily taken with whatever newfangledness was in front of him. I watched him go from being engrossed by books, to the theater, to fatherhood, back to bachelorhood and the narcissisms of exercise, to rock climbing, and now he was accessorizing as a hippie-come-lately: he grew his hair long, donned his Birkenstocks, a hemp necklace, and started wearing shorts and flowery shirts to work, where he held a job as a technical writer at a software company. I don't wish to seem to my learned reader that I was or am in any way judgmental of Luke. Even though his transformation was so rapid as to seem insincere, I didn't doubt Luke's genuineness. I was delighted by his assimilation into my world of song and dance. On several occasions when incredibly baked, drifting across boundaries of time like my grandmother, I found Charlie's disembodied voice saying, *You've got to be a cow, motherfucker! A cow doesn't try to be a cow. It's just a cow. It just does what a cow does.* I was just doing what I thought I needed to do: let go and forget, and Luke had decided he was joining me on the voyage.

I'd started writing a few stories again and selling them to magazines—not for any serious amount of money, but mainly to cushion the scraps of the abysmal part-time-instructor pay I was making at the various two-year colleges around Charlotte. What the colleges lacked in compensation they made up for in fringe benefits, and I was seeing more than my fair share of fringes—so much that Luke had actually taken me aside one evening and laid down the law for me:

"I don't care who you fuck, just don't fuck them in my bed."

I nodded, feigning remorse.

"Or my brother's bed either."

"Well, where exactly—"

"Fuck 'em on the floor, fuck 'em on the couch—I don't care. I don't like getting in my bed at night feeling a mildly

damp spot from where you were banging some chick earlier in the day."

"What about the stairs?"

"Fine, whatever," Luke said.

As far as I was concerned, life was headed back into calm
waters. It felt the same as the old days: Luke and me kicking
back—his brother, Dick, was there, but he was essentially
harmless—having a chance to get it right this time. The
angst and anxiety I'd harbored for years was replaced by another level—a level where I found contentment in the un-
folding of the day, eating when hungry, sleeping when tired,
and in between those activities and my profession (which
revolved around the construction of the five-paragraph es-
say), getting absolutely baked and feeling the flow of the
music.

We decided to drive to Wisconsin on Memorial Day weekend in 2002, to attend an annual festival put on by the Big
Wu. I'd moved out of Luke's place by this time because his
brother and I had some personal differences. The name of
that difference was Mirabelle. She'd been Dick's best friend
through high school, and I came to understand later that he
was desperately in love with her—and who could blame
him? She was a bubbly girl with a mesmerizing smile and
the most prolific tits I'd seen outside of a magazine. Upon
seeing her for the first time I was immediately reminded of a
boating-safety course I took when I was twelve—I was certain that I remembered how to properly use a flotation
safety device. But at the time I wasn't concerned about
Dick—I was trying to save myself from drowning. I'm sure

it didn't help matters when I decided I needed Mirabelle to rescue me in his bed one evening while he was out delivering pizzas.

Luke, Dick, Mirabelle, and I drove to Madison, Wisconsin, and met my friend Cassandra; she'd flown in from New York. From there we drove the two hours to Black River Falls, a small town on the border with Minnesota where the festival was being held.

Roughly three thousand people had turned out for two days of music in the Wisconsin woods. Huddles of tents spiraled from the fields into the thicket of trees like giant Day-Glo toadstools. People had set up camp chairs around fires, grills sent the smell of meat and portobello mushrooms and eggplant circling through the air, and the rhythmic thunder of tribal drums echoed from every direction. As we walked through the tent villages, the scent of weed was heavy in the air, and every so often a bearded young man toting a backpack would pass by us quietly chanting his wares: *Nugs, 'shrooms, doses, rolls . . . all super kind . . .*

It was paradise—it was the lost world I'd been in search of. No worries, no regrets. We were in the woods in a temporary autonomous zone, and soon good music was going to come cascading from the field a few hundred yards away.

We'd barely gotten our tents staked when a kid in scraggly clothes cruised into our camp.

"What's happening?" he said.

"It's all good," I said. "What's happening with you, brother?" Something about being gathered together in a forest with other individuals experiencing the wonders of group consciousness had me and nearly everyone else talking like extras from a remake of *Dobie Gillis*.

"I'm just sharing in the groove," he said, nodding his head to a music only he could hear.

"Cool," I said.

Cassandra walked up beside me.

"Hey, hey, pretty mama," the kid said.

"Hey, yourself. So what you got for me?" Cassandra shot back.

The kid's eyes lit up, and he patted the pockets on the sides of his cargo pants.

"Why don't we step into my laboratory," I said, pronouncing *laboratory* as a mad scientist might in a cheap monster movie.

"Cool, cool," the kid said.

We all shuffled into the tent-gazebo we'd bought for general hanging-out purposes; Luke had been fiddling around with the flap of his personal tent, but once he saw that we were engaged in business, he quickly joined us.

The kid took out several bags of mushrooms from one of his pockets, and from his other pocket at least an ounce of the dankest bud I'd laid eyes on since leaving Syracuse.

"I'll take that," I said, indicating the weed.

"How much you want, man?"

"All of it."

"Sheee-it! Right the fuck on. That's three bills." I gave the kid the three hundred bucks, picked up the bag of weed, opened it, and pressed my face in.

I've often gotten a great deal of enjoyment from mocking the way oenophiles prance about their beloved vintage du jour, swirling their glass, thrusting their noses in, then taking the most prissy sip, but with a bag of finely grown cannabis I have to turn the lens of ridicule upon myself.

I'd closed my eyes, breathing deeply, and when I looked up, everyone was staring at me and the kid's smile was spangled across his entire face.

"That is the funky-funky space antelope shit. You know it! You know it!" And he stuck out his hand for me to slap him five. "Now, who's looking for the diggity fungus?"

The weed had broken the bank for me, and that was fine. I made it a point to avoid psychedelics. While I'd been feeling more or less grounded for the past two years, I didn't know how much I wanted to test my boundaries. Besides, my friend Milo, who is rather a connoisseur in matters of mind-altering chemicals, said to me at the Trey Anastasio show in Asheville in March of 2001, "Dude, that weed has done wonders for you, but if you ever try acid or 'shrooms, best make sure there's a straitjacket and some haloperidol available."

Luke and Cassandra each purchased an eighth of mushrooms from the kid; the 'shrooms were streaked with white and purple: a good sign. When the kid had finished packing up his wares, he said to Luke and Cassandra, "Now, listen . . ." His tone had shifted; he sounded exceptionally parental. "This is not to be fucked around with. Eat a cap, maybe a stem, but *stop there*. I repeat, *do not go balls out*. Assess the situation. Proceed with caution." He stood up and smiled at us all, then began a little jig, a slithering, fluid wave that passed up from his legs and through hips and arms, then down again, and as he danced, he floated right out of the camp. We gave one another the eye, and finally Luke's brother stepped into the tent and said, "Well, what the fuck was that about?"

It was nearly June, but it was also Wisconsin, and it

suddenly turned cold and began to drizzle. We spent the rest of the night huddled around a piss-poor fire, listening as the bands played to a soaked crowd in the field at the top of the hill. Eventually I wandered into my tent and surfed the edge of a high semi-slumber, and then Cassandra and Mirabelle came into the tent and lay on either side of me—it was a deep, pleasing sleep that finally took me down.

The woods were wreathed in smoke and fog when we woke the next morning. I imagined an English encampment long ago on St. Crispin's Day, the wearied warriors waiting for their king to rouse them to battle. People sopped through the boggy path in front of our tents that had become a small tributary when the rain had picked up during the night. My mood was exactly that of someone wet and cold about to face a hundred Frenchmen with broadswords. I walked back out to the field where the cars were parked, found mine, turned it on, and waited for it to heat up. I tuned the radio to the local NPR station. Cassandra and Mirabelle soon tracked me down and joined me in the car's warmth, and we all sat not speaking, getting stoned, and listening to Michael Feldman quiz his audience.

After lunch the sun came out and Luke and Cassandra decided the turn in the weather was enough to justify their partaking of the mushrooms. They each ate a cap and a stem, as advised, while the rest of us tried to see just how stoned we could get. To say that we were flat-fucked baked shitless would be a mild understatement.

We walked up to the field in front of the stage. The first band of the day was coming on—Olospo, a group from somewhere in Texas. Absolutely incredible. The five of us lay on our backs reading the hieroglyphics of the clouds, though occasionally one or two of us would be so swayed by the pure funk the band was laying down that we had to rise and spin around and flail our arms nonsensically.

At some point Luke said, "I've got to take a walk." When someone is five sheets to the wind and he feels it necessary to walk, it means his buzz is taking him in a direction he doesn't want to go, and the walking is an effort to get back on the right path.

"I'll walk with you," I said, and Luke and I weaved our way back toward the forest; clouds with bellies like wild river water were rollicking on the horizon, and the woods had given rise early to shadows that slunk around the bases of the trees.

"What's going on in your head?" I asked Luke.

"Not much, baby, not much." I wasn't sure I believed him. "I kind of peaked a while back. I'm cool. I just needed to walk."

"That's cool." We chattered about the band as we made our way down the path toward our tents. Someone's camp-fire was huffing smoke in billows across the path, and out of the smoke emerged a young kid with a goatee and his hair gelled up so that it looked like horns. Luke reached out and grabbed my arm hard enough that his nails pinched me.

"Ow, fuck!"

"What the fuck, dude?" He wasn't letting go of my arm. "What the fuck was that?"

"That dude?"

"Fuck that dude, man. I'm talking about that *fucking demon.*"

"Uh, that was a guy with his hair gelled up, Luke."

"It was? You sure?"

"Luke, get a grip. Other than my arm." I pried his fingers from my biceps. "It was just some guy. Besides, you don't believe in devils, demons, God, or any of that shit."

"Yeah, yeah, you're right. I don't . . ." He peered nervously from side to side.

When we reached our camp, Luke said, "I'm going to just chill for a minute in my tent. That cool?"

"Fine with me. I'm going to go take a leak. You'll be okay?"

"I'm okay." He smiled wearily.

I didn't go back to the camp immediately after my excursion into the bowels of the Porta-John; I had to wash my hands. A return to craziness? You'd be crazy *not* to want to bathe in rubbing alcohol and peroxide after an experience like that. As it turned out, the "hand washing station" was on the complete opposite side of the festival grounds, and so I tromped off in search of cleanliness. The hand washing station was merely a faucet activated by a foot pump, and the water that drained out of the sink was circulated through a filter and redistributed back onto one's hands; how wonderfully thoughtful for the earth, but this was seriously testing how far away from the crazies I'd moved in the last two years. I decided I hadn't moved far enough and went over to one of the vending trailers that all day long cooked up vegan items that looked and tasted like meat. I knocked on the door on the far end of the trailer. No one answered at first, so I knocked again, louder.

A girl with beautiful blonde dreadlocks opened the door. She eyed me suspiciously and said, "Gotta wait in line like everyone else, sweetie." She started to close the door.

"Wait. I have a proposition for you?"

She opened the door back up and looked at me with raised eyebrows. "Oh?"

"I know this is going to sound absolutely insane, but I'll give you five dollars if you let me wash my hands."

"You're right. That does sound insane. I would've let you wash them for a dollar, but you're in for five now."

I was happy to pay the five. Happy and clean.

When I got back to the camp, the others had returned; Luke was sitting in a lounge chair, laughing to himself, his pupils like black holes.

"What's with him?" I said to the group.

"I don't know," Cassandra said, "but he must have gotten a different batch than I did—I'm feeling good, but he's *zonked.*"

"He's fine. But I think I could be slightly more baked. Anyone?" Mirabelle followed me back into the tent where the bong was stashed. We passed it back and forth at least ten times before we heard the howl.

Time wasn't operating at its normal pace for Mirabelle and me, so I can't say how long we sat there staring at one another before the commotion grew to such a level that I said, "I think I'd better check on that."

"Yeah," she said.

At first I thought Luke had fallen into the fire; he was rolling around on the ground clawing at his face. His brother was screaming, "Luke! Luke! Luke!"

I ran over and looked at Cassandra. "What happened?"

Cassandra was sitting in the corner of the communal tent, her eyes wide, shaking her head. I could tell this was going to be a disastrous waste of a buzz. "Dick," I said. "What happened?"

Dick wasn't listening to me. He was freaking out, grabbing Luke by the arms and trying to restrain him, but then I saw why: Luke was tearing out clumps of his hair and attempting to eat dirt. Fortunately, Dick was strong enough to hold Luke—Luke is a big guy, six feet four at least and naturally muscular; Dick is built the same way—but I have to chalk it up to adrenaline that he was able to overcome his brother's thrashing. I got down next to Luke and said, "Luke, it's Keck. Look at me, Luke. Everything is cool. You're with people who care, everything is going to be just fine."

"*You're freaking out on drugs, Luke! You've overdosed but we'll save you!*" Dick was screaming just inches from Luke's face; I squeezed Dick's shoulder and got his attention long enough to indicate that he should cut that amateur-hour bullshit out right away.

"Luke, ignore your brother. Everything is cool—you're just having a moment."

Luke was looking back and forth between his brother and me; he had the look of alarm reminiscent of Charlton Heston's when he's taken captive by speaking apes. For all I knew, he thought we were apes.

Luke hadn't said anything coherent thus far. He was moaning and mumbling syllables, but nothing close to words. If Dick let him go, he'd start to thrash about. So

Dick held him still while I repeated my mantra of coolness: "Everything is fine, Luke, everything is cool. This'll pass. This is temporary."

Occasionally passersby would stop and try to intervene, offering sentiments designed to instantly soothe Luke, and also position them as professionals when it came to negotiating the territory of psychedelic experiences. In nearly every instance these were teenagers or kids in their early twenties, and once they caught a good look at Luke's face, distorted in a grimace of terror and total alienation, they went about their business rather quickly. The people closer to our age kept moving when they spotted the scene of Luke, and one guy even said to me, "Good luck with that one, pal," and he shook his head as if remembering his own voyage into the dark regions.

Suddenly Luke began to speak, and, friends, let me tell you: I can't come close to getting you to understand what I witnessed. To this day I don't know what it was, and I will go to my grave marveling over it. Imagine if you took all the words in your vocabulary and somehow shook them up in your head until they were completely jumbled, then began to speak them as fast as you could, without hesitation, and as though this were your native tongue. It was like watching James Joyce fuck Thomas Pynchon on an electric fence while they were both suffering an epileptic seizure during a fit of Tourette's. I have tried numerous times to re-create Luke's gushing of archetypal imagery, and I have never been successful. But you must believe me: this stands as one of the most bizarre and amazing things I've ever seen in person.

Jesus fucking Christ, I thought, *I don't know if I'm qualified to handle this.* All those *After School Specials* were beginning to seem more credible. I wondered if Luke could hear the sound of sizzling eggs in his brain.

And just as quickly as he'd launched into his muddled monologue, he quit. He looked at his brother and said, "You're Dick."

"Everything's going to be okay, Luke. You've just hit a rough spot."

"*What the fuck is a penis?*" Luke screamed. I looked around. A lot of people had turned their attention our way.

I heard the sound of a motorized vehicle pulling up behind me; I began to assess how I would explain this to the authorities—Dick was the weak link; he'd start babbling. But it was too late to put a steel spike through his head; even so, I refocused my thoughts. Now was not the time for bad vibes. I had to maintain. The course of the evening was in my hands.

Two paramedics knelt beside me.

"This your friend?" one of them said.

"Yes. He's going through a tough time. I think we've got it under control."

"Are you Jesus?" Luke asked the other paramedic. The paramedics gave each other the fish eye.

"Okay, look," I said to the first paramedic in my most confessional tone, "he's had some mushrooms. This is not something he's used to. I think he's had a panic attack that along with the mushrooms has caused a temporary psychosis, but unless you're prepared to administer a tranquilizer for him, I doubt there's much more that you can do that I'm not already doing, which is talking this poor bastard out of the hole he's in. Do what you gotta do, but let's try not to aggravate what's already a fragile situation."

"Understood. I'm just going to check his vitals."

Either the medic had taken a fair share of drugs himself or he'd seen enough in his time on the job that he knew I was shooting straight with him. The worst element that can be introduced to a negative psychotropic experience is an ignorant participant with a fear of the unknown. There was no way of telling how Dick's anxiety had impacted Luke, but I suppose he was doing the best he knew how. As much as I wanted to, I couldn't fault him for over-reacting.

The medic was good. He gently pressed Luke's wrist and told him that things were totally under control and that he was in a safe place with people who were looking out for him. He moved a small light back and forth in front of Luke's eyes, then said, "Do you know your name?"

"What is Wisconsin?" Luke pleaded.

The medic looked back at me. "Man, this guy is fucked up."

"So I'm not responsible for anything I've ever done? No. That's not right. Is my hand my penis?" Luke was twisting his head around, gazing at everything and nothing.

The medic looked at Luke again, then stood. "Well, call us if you need us. But you should probably get him out of sight, if you know what I mean." I didn't imagine there were too many ways of interpreting that, so as the medics left, Dick and I talked Luke to his feet, then helped him into the tent and put him in a folding chair. I had Mirabelle cut up some oranges and feed them to Luke to get his blood sugar back in line and bring the high down. Finally, Luke looked at me and said, "Are you bisexual?"

"Mirabelle, feed the man more oranges. He's out of his head."

It rained again that night, a ferocious downpour that splattered mud on everything and caused the dying fires to hiss and pop in the soaked darkness. Luke was (quite understandably) having a little trouble settling down for the night, so he and I sat in the gazebo tent, taking turns tending the fire to avoid the bitch of starting it from scratch with wet wood in the morning.

Neither of us was really saying much. There was some idle chatter about this song or that song that drifted down the hill and managed to be audible above the pressing rain, but mainly we just watched the fire.

"So, Luke, what the fuck happened?"

"Well, I guess I should preface this by saying that when you left to go piss, I took some more."

"Aha! I knew it! You dumb motherfucker—no offense, I'm glad you're okay—but rule number one of consuming drugs: when the person selling the drugs tells you to be cautious, *be fucking cautious*. It's not meant to be a marketing tactic. The dude is honestly trying to spare you exactly what happened."

"I know, I know . . ."

"But, seriously, what was going on in your head? You were totally AWOL, man. I'm not going to lie to you: there was a moment . . ." I didn't feel like finishing. Luke knew where I was headed with that statement.

He stared into the fire; I wasn't completely convinced he was totally himself. "It was weird, Keck. I ceased to exist. I wasn't Luke. I knew there was no death, that everything continued and was everything—I was guided by spheres of light that were singing; I knew they were angels. The world as we see it is not the world as it is. I felt if I wanted to see God, God was ready to reveal himself—or herself; I'm not sure, you know, because it wasn't like a person, you know? It was a . . . I don't know how to explain it. It was all-encompassing, it was just more love than I've ever known, and I was scared because I knew I couldn't be Luke anymore if I wanted to be with God, and the part of me that is Luke, the most unreal part, because the ego is just this illusion, but it's strong and I wasn't ready. I had to be Luke"—here he looked at me—"and I'm just so absolutely sad about it."

I believed him. He looked positively forlorn, but I also knew that a rough trip could unsettle you for hours and days afterward—longer in extreme cases—and I figured his mood would pass. I felt I'd at least tasted what he was talking about. In a few instances I have smoked pot as a precursor to deep meditation. (Serious practitioners of meditation will tell you that's a bad idea, and I agree with them wholeheartedly. However, I am a serious pot smoker, not the other way around, and so I choose to shoot the moon however it pleases me.) During one of these meditation sessions I seemed to travel to a level of consciousness where I felt I stood on the edge of selflessness—the archer taking aim at oneself and becoming an unmoved center, the bow uniting heaven and earth, and the string sounding the perfect tone of unison.

But because I'd cheated my way there, much as Luke

had, the sensation alarmed me and I came out of my trance in an absolute panic—I'd come as close as I'd ever come to knowing what it was to not be Kevin Keck, to not having a sense of anything. *It's just being a cow, motherfucker!* I'd wanted to call Charlie after that and ask him if that was what he meant, this notion of just being, but by the next morning my question seemed frivolous and so I never bothered to ask. Charlie had always talked about theology and desire—that something within us could only fundamentally be explained and given meaning by the innate desire to connect with others and ourselves through a theological lens—all this business of psychoanalysis and philosophy was just a part of the equation, but it was ultimately destined to be a kind of "disappointment of thinking."

Once, in the bar of the Sheraton Hotel, while waiting to take my shot during a game of pool, I wandered over to where Charlie was sitting sipping on his glass of wine, and I asked him straight out, "Charlie, do you believe in God?"

"Do I believe in a magical man floating on a cloud who tallies the prayers of the infirmed? No." And he took one of those great, dramatic drags from his Basic Ultra Light 100. "But do I believe in a god? Of course I do."

I wish I'd been smart enough to explain to Luke what Charlie might have to say about this experience of his, but I wasn't. This was something that Charlie would have to explain, and he couldn't. Charlie had died the month before.

Exodus

My bad luck at the Baptist college extended to my next few teaching gigs—ultimately I wound up at an art school, and the bad luck there had a name: Lilith. I foolishly decided to take a chance on love (or at the very least, lust), and thus a few months after my dismissal from the art school my life took a disastrous turn—I'd opted to indulge a fantasy that if I returned to the simplicity of making pizzas, as I'd done during the summer of 1994, then I would regain that blissful state of being that I'd possessed in those days before I went completely bonkers. I got a job at Domino's. I'd been on the job for a week when I assessed that (1) I was being supervised by a twenty-four-year-old guy who had failed to graduate high school and was routinely showing up late because he played video games until four in the morning; (2) I had a master's degree and was making $7.50 an hour; (3) I'd rather be living out of my car than putting up with the minutiae of counting exactly the right amount of pepperoni on a large pizza so that the food inventory balanced at the end of the night.

Thus, by midspring, I was living out of my car.

One night in a fit of nostalgia I got it in my head that if I could somehow reconnect with Lilith—who'd deserted me as soon as I was reduced in rank from professer to pizza baker—I might begin to find my way again. I drove to her apartment—it was probably around nine or ten at night. Naturally I hadn't bothered to call first, and as I turned the corner to park in front of her building, there she stood, all five feet two inches of her, coal black hair billowing in the slight breeze, swept up in a deeply passionate kiss from a tattooed gentleman twice my size.

Of course, as my headlights beamed across them, they broke their embrace and gazed at my car as I passed; I tried not to look, but out of the corner of my eye Lilith appeared puzzled and surprised—*obviously*. I drove past them and to the edge of the parking lot where a Chevy Blazer shielded me in my Kia Sephia. How was I to face her as she was enfolded in the well-muscled arms of some stagish brute when I drove a four-cylinder economy car with a rhyming name?

There was no other way out of the parking lot. I turned off the ignition and stayed in the car. I rolled down a window and listened for voices: nothing. I thought I heard footsteps and so I waited for the thuggish gentleman to approach my car and politely inquire as to the nature of my fucking problem.

I should perhaps mention that I was, as Morrison said, *stoned immaculate*. In fact, I was a little *too stoned*. I was suddenly overwhelmed with the sensation that I was a finite being. The terror was absolute, and I felt as though I were going stark raving mad. I needed to get out of that car. Suddenly I became jittery; I could feel my heart in my throat, and then I couldn't. *WAIT! Where's my heart?* I searched frantically for my pulse, and yet I knew I was still breathing. *I'm going to die, I'm going to die, I'm going to die, I am a tiny being alone in the universe, my God, get me out of this car!*

But I wasn't getting out of the car. I waited for what felt like an hour, then cranked the engine. I looked at the digital clock on the dash as it was illuminated: only five minutes had actually passed. I said, *Well, the humiliation can't get any worse*, and turned on the radio: Warren Zevon—always the bard to best brace one for failure. Lilith and her man watched me as I drove past. I didn't bother to wave.

I turned the radio up: *Well, he's just an excitable boy . . .* I rolled the windows down. I could smell the world blossoming again and I couldn't breathe it in deeply enough; I never wanted my life to leave me. The lights from the city were washing out all the stars, and I needed to see the stars—my heart was nearly leaping from my throat, and I wanted to find a cool patch of grass and gaze at the stars and find a sense of something greater than myself.

I was headed in the direction of my parents' house, but when their driveway appeared, I kept on driving. Within two miles I'd reached the intersection of Denver proper. The town I'm from is not even technically a town. It lost its state charter the year I was born because it couldn't generate enough tax revenue. Now it was an unzoned free-for-all for carpetbaggers and scalawags to layer their apportioned land with those accursed mini-warehouses, cheap strip-mall shopping centers that housed nail salons and Christian bookstores, and used-car lots. Every church was the same bland Protestant brick rectangle, as though one of Martin Luther's theses had encouraged a new Christianity of boredom. But there was at least one holy place in Denver.

I parked my car in the shadows along the edge of a newly paved entrance to a housing development, and then I walked down Will Proctor Street toward the darkened rows of buildings across the road: Rock Spring Camp Ground.

The campground isn't what you think: it doesn't host RVs or tents, but is instead two square rings of wooden-slatted cabins that are referred to as tents. Most of them have electricity, though some don't. All of them have a water supply, but not every one has a toilet, and thus many people still employ the reliable technology of the chamber pot. In the center of the campground is an open-air sanctuary.

Each tent bears a number and is owned by one family or another, and they are passed down from generation to generation. To own one of these tents places a family in a hierarchy, members of a bloodline with an interest rooted in the history of the area. For two weeks out of the year, always in August, people come to the campground (some from thousands of miles away) and stay in the tents, passing the hot August afternoons by going to the lake or playing cards (never gambling), and at night listening for the sound of the bell in the arbor to call them to worship. Because of the way the population was spread out in the area in the eighteenth and nineteenth centuries, it was difficult to organize a sustainable church, and as the area was mostly agricultural, people couldn't just leave their fields unattended. The camp meeting began in 1794 as a way to bring people together for worship on a grand scale, and it's been at its present location since 1830. I suspect it will be there until an act of God displaces it, because the people of Denver would only accept that level of authority when it comes to the campground.

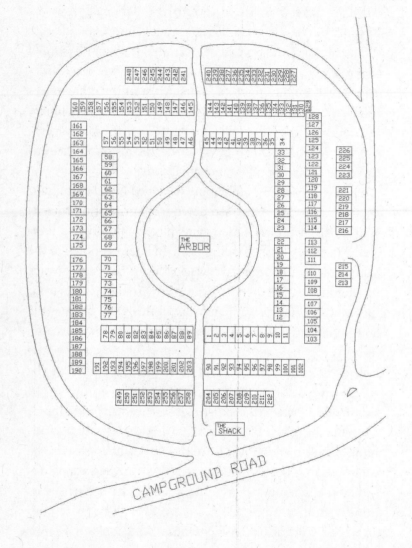

THE ARBOR

THE SHACK

CAMPGROUND ROAD

I only know of one other: Tucker's Grove. It's situated a few miles away and is in decline, which is a terrible thing. But what is more terrible is the reason there are two camp-grounds: if you were to join me on a walk around Rock Spring Camp Ground on a humid August night when the people are sitting in their porch swings and greeting their neighbors with brotherly and motherly love, you might notice one peculiar thing—all those people are white. Because of the time when camp meeting began, it is understandable that there were segregated places of worship, but for reasons I've failed to grasp no one has seen fit to heal this rift.

My family doesn't own a tent at the campground, so I can't claim to have grown up with my summers marked by this annual communion, but I did spend some glorious August nights here.

Tent 57: that's where you would've found me. It's where the Blackmon family spent their time, and a choice spot: right on the corner, and right across from two paths, one taking you beyond the outer realm of the campground, the other taking you to its heart (although in reality every tent on that inner rectangle has a door that opens onto the arbor). Toby Blackmon and I became good friends when I began to ride the same school bus that he rode; he obviously rode it because it went by his house—I rode it because it went *near* my house, and the incredibly large fellow who was nineteen and still in the eleventh grade wasn't on it to beat my ass. My previous bus may have dropped me at my door, but it wasn't worth the price of the convenience.

I suppose Toby and I got along initially because he was also a bookish fellow who liked science fiction. I gave up on *Star Trek* in high school when I discovered it didn't allow for me to set my penis on stun. But before all that Toby was my boon companion, and the summer I was sixteen he suggested that I join his family during camp meeting.

I'd grown up hearing about camp meeting, but I didn't know much about it. All I gleaned was that it was some sort of religious festival that made all my friends disappear for two weeks. What it turned out to be was a magnificent social event of the most humble sort, minus the alcohol.

But at the age of sixteen I had yet to reach the point where social occasions must be softened with a drink. It was just a splendid expression of communal goodwill. Everyone I knew from school was there, and plenty of people I didn't know, and nearly everyone was with his or her family, so there was no disguising who you were and where you came from. It was a coming together to shed the artifice of self as one's sins were shed before Christ.

The religious aspect of camp meeting was mainly taken up by those in attendance who had squared away their marital options. The young and single typically did one thing: they walked. The walking loop of the campground, between the inner and outer rectangles of tents, was a promenade of hopeful courting, as famous to the people of Denver as Atlantic City's boardwalk.

I made my way to tent 57. The swings had been hauled inside and it was locked, the same as any other tent. What the fuck was I doing here anyway? There really weren't too many places for me to go besides home. I'd burned the bridge with a mighty blaze in my last living arrangement, sticking my roommate with two months of past-due rent. I'd made a Hail Mary attempt to salvage that situation after I quit the pizza place: I tried selling pot, forgetting William

Burroughs's wise insight that selling reefer is like farming frogs—it makes sense on paper. Especially if you're using that paper to roll up fat joints and smoking all your profits, and so I'd ended up owing a dealer roughly five hundred dollars. It wasn't *that serious*—weed isn't like cocaine; no one is going to come and shoot you over five hundred dollars. On a certain level it's slightly worse: when you owe a weed dealer money, he shows up at your house every day and spends an hour giving you a guilt trip about being responsible. At some point a bullet in the knee would be a welcome change. I finally went to my grandfather and told him I'd screwed up and borrowed money from the wrong people. My grandfather was not a man to frivolously lend money, but he also believed in the bonds of family, and if someone had an ass-kicking coming to him, by God it was going to be dealt out by blood and not by strangers. I'd promised to pay him fifty dollars a week until we were square; six weeks had gone by and I hadn't paid him anything.

I walked around the corner of the tent and toward the arbor. I'd almost forgotten my intentions: a cool patch of grass and a canopy of stars. I flopped down on the ground and looked at the speckles of light stretching along the black blanket above me.

On the last night of camp meeting during the August of 1991, Jeremy, Gary, Madge, Misty, and I left the campground an hour before the sun went down. Gary had a bottle of rum, and Jeremy and I had brought along some beer we'd stolen from our respective fathers: Schaefer Light from me, and Michelob from Jeremy. Although my dad to this day will claim that Schaefer was the finest of brews in his youth, I was not greeted as the great deliverer of spoils that night. We took separate cars: Gary's and mine. Gary had a Dodge Daytona—Madge was happy to ride with him. Jeremy and Misty rode in my car, which was how I wanted it: Jeremy had an angle on Misty, but I was playing for the same angle, and so I wanted to ensure they weren't left alone.

We drove south on Highway 16 and then turned east on 73. We were headed out to the old quarry that was flooded when the river was dammed for the hydroelectric station in 1962.

You reached the old quarry by parking at an apartment complex, crossing a thin line of pines, then following an old service road that eventually slithered between two ponds and gnarled maples that stood stout and twisted, their limbs grappling with one another so that you had to duck slightly to pass through. The brush seemed to close in around the path and it grew darker, and as you turned to your left thinking that you were surely reaching an impassable point, the trees and underbrush opened miraculously onto a bluff that overlooked the two nuclear reactor buildings nearly half a mile away on the opposite shore.

There was already a well-worn black spot in the middle of the cliff where bonfires were lit weekly. The only view of the point where we stood was from the nuclear plant itself, and the security guards most likely found more pleasure in surveying us with their binoculars than reporting us to the local police.

By the time we got to the cliff the beer had turned too warm for anyone but me and Gary, and so Jeremy and the girls passed the bottle of Bacardi 151 back and forth as we all took turns trying our hand at a fire—which is surprisingly hard even when you do have a lighter. I was carrying some folded-up paper in my pockets—poems I'd written that were derivative drivel. Jeremy had put his arm around Misty, and so I made a long speech about the nature of being an artist and destroying work that was forever irretrievable.

"So read them to us," Misty said.

I quickly began to ball the poems up for kindling.

"No, seriously," she said, propelling herself from under Jeremy's arm and to her feet. She grabbed one of the pieces of paper from my hand before I had a chance to hold it out of her reach.

But what Misty read was about her—I make no claim about its greatness; I know that I was still using words such as *thee* and *thou* in my poetry. But I was young. What did I know of poetry?

I'd stooped down to try to get the fire started finally, when Jeremy stood and snatched the poem from Misty's hand, glanced at it quickly, then crumpled it and chucked it onto the small pile of twigs.

"Good job, Kevin," he said. "You got the fire going."

Misty fished in her pockets for a cigarette.

"Dude," Gary said, "get on this beer. If it gets any hotter we're gonna yak."

I downed a Schaefer quickly, then another, and it is not a beverage to be consumed at any temperature other than ice-cold. We passed trivial conversation back and forth until we arrived at the topic of our imminent departures, all of which would be happening over the next few weeks.

Gary, Misty, and Madge were all headed to Chapel Hill. Jeremy was going to UNC-Charlotte.

"What the fuck makes you want to go there?" Gary asked.

"I'm not paying for it," Jeremy said. We already knew Jeremy wasn't paying for it. His dad was on disability from the Korean War; his parents had met in an asylum.

"When do you leave, Kevin?" Madge asked. Madge and I had lived a mile from one another for several years, but we'd only hung out a few times.

I was headed to Belmont Abbey, a Catholic college, even though I was about as far from being Catholic as I was from being Chinese.

"I leave at the end of next week," I said.

"Man," Gary said, "you are going to get fucked up there." He wasn't speaking in terms of twisted theology; the Abbey had a grand reputation as a party school. One of our local saints, Doug Rice, had managed to drink his way through the Abbey for two semesters and emerge with a grade point average of untransferable proportions. I was confident in my ability to outlast Doug.

"It's a cool place," I said, "and at least there I won't be a number like you guys at Chapel Hill."

"Yeah," Gary said, "but your basketball team will suck." He whipped his beer can over the ledge.

"You know you just want to have your cock sucked by a priest," Jeremy said. "That's what goes on at those Catholic schools."

"I'm more interested in the Catholic girls."

"Yeah, I think we all know better."

I whipped my beer can at Jeremy's head. "Shut the fuck up," I said. Jeremy looked at me and smirked; it was his secret as much as mine.

Misty was standing close to the edge of the cliff, staring down at an outcropping of rocks where the cliff sloped down and cradled a cove. "I want to go down to those rocks," she said. "Kevin, walk me down? It's dark."

I didn't make eye contact with Jeremy, but instead stood up and stumbled over to Misty, who was already headed in the direction of the trail. "Someone should keep the fire going," I said to no one in particular as she and I disappeared.

We walked for a long time in silence, and at some point she seemed to stumble close to me and press her body into mine. We continued walking that way, and ultimately the Schaefer gave me courage enough to wrap my arm around her; she was wearing a denim jacket over a tank top, and I found her hand in her pocket; I wrapped my fingers around her fist.

When we reached the rocks that jutted out from the cove, Misty pulled away from me, kicked off her shoes, and waded out a few feet to where another rock rose from the water. "They've got the fire going good," she said. "You can really see it from here."

It seemed like a pain in the ass to take my shoes and socks off, wade in the water, then wade back and not have a towel handy to dry my feet. I didn't like the idea of getting my feet dirty.

"What are you afraid of?"

"I'm not afraid of anything," I said, but Misty didn't respond. I saw the silhouette of her head turn from me back toward the cliff again.

Misty lit her cigarette and stood staring up at the fire on the cliff; I picked up a stone and tried to skip it across the water. Several months ago I couldn't have imagined finding myself in this situation with Misty. We'd gone to school together since second grade, and we'd usually been in a lot of the same classes, but we'd never said much to each other. Which is not to say we didn't get along—we did, but I was also the kid who wore suspenders to school nearly every day between eighth and tenth grade. I was most often classified as wacky, and wacky didn't get you laid. At least not until college when you started hanging out with theater chicks with eating disorders. But toward the end of the school year Misty and I had started hanging out, taking drives to the record store, things like that. I discovered in that short time that she and I thought more alike than I'd ever realized, and that of all the people who I believed were on my frequency, she really was, and somehow I'd missed it all those years.

"What are you thinking of?" Misty asked, still perched on her rock, out of my reach across the shallows.

"I don't know."

"You're always thinking of something."

"I suppose I was thinking about what's under all this water."

I couldn't see Misty's face, but I had the feeling she was looking me over with cool skepticism. "Why would you be thinking that?"

"I don't know. I heard a lot of towns were lost when they built the dam. Beatties Ford Road used to go from Charlotte to Davidson, but it's somewhere under the lake now. Revolutionary battle sites, Civil War battle sites . . . it's just forgotten under the water."

"I can't imagine you were thinking anything of the sort."

I didn't have a response, and so I just stood there, alternately contemplating the reactors across the cove and the fire burning on the bluff.

I heard Misty's cigarette hiss in the water, then the soft splashes as she waded back to the shore. She put her hand on my shoulder and lifted each foot, brushing off the bottoms, then sliding her shoes back on. When she was done, she said, "Why did you decide on Belmont Abbey?"

"I don't really know." I knew. I knew good and well why I'd made that decision, but I was too embarrassed to say.

"I think you know, but I think you're afraid to say."

I started to protest, but before I could begin to formulate a response Gary, Jeremy, and Madge had started to scream up on the cliff. At first it sounded like distress, but then I realized it was exuberance.

"What are they doing up there?" Misty asked, and I turned around just in time to see a figure emerge as if from the fire itself and leap over the edge of the cliff. Misty clutched my arm.

And then Jeremy's voice burst from the water, unmistakable and triumphant—*defiant*.

"Wooo! Take *that*, fuckers! I am *unstoppable*! Wooooo!" In an instant Misty let go of my arm, kicked off her shoes, threw her pack of cigarettes and lighter on the ground, and went running into the water, taking a few strides and then gracefully falling forward into a gleeful swim toward Jeremy. I wasn't going to be *that guy* waiting on the shore. I shook a cigarette out of Misty's pack, lit it, then began the hike back up to the cliff. By the time I got to the top Gary was pouring the few remaining beers over the fire.

"I think that might have been too much, man," Gary said. "I thought I saw a patrol boat cruising the channel."

"You're just being paranoid," Madge said.

"Yeah, well, this beer sucks, it's warm, and I'm ready to head back. This is lame."

"What got into Jeremy?" I asked.

"You know how Jeremy is," Madge said.

"Crazy bastard," Gary said. He was clearly impressed.

"Misty jumped in the water after him," I said as casually as possible.

"Well, yeah," Gary said. "Like no one saw that coming. Anyway, the fire's out. Let's split."

Back at the campground a lot of the teenagers were sprawled on blankets and lawn chairs on the area just around the arbor, near the corner and tent 57. The Perseid meteor shower was at its peak that night, and by the time Jeremy and Misty had dried off and we'd all reached the lawn, the sky was streaked with streams of white light.

No one really said anything for the longest time, and finally I noticed that Madge and Gary were gone; Jeremy was asleep, and Misty was lying close to him, staring up at the shooting stars. I raised my eyes to the spectacle again; I was running out of wishes to make.

"Kevin," Misty said, almost a whisper, "I know why you're going." She didn't say anything for a moment, and I thought she'd spoken to me from a dream she was having. But then she said, "You need to be close to this."

I was starting to itch from the grass, and quite honestly I was pretty drained. I wanted someplace comfortable to lay my head, but I didn't want to go home. When I was fleeing under cover of darkness from my last apartment, deciding which possessions were crucial and which could be left behind, I'd called Luke in the hope that the couch might still be available.

"I don't know, Keck. I just feel like we're moving in different directions. You know, I'm keeping Kiley more these days, and quite honestly my brother really doesn't like you. He's pretty much said that he would rather drag his eyeball along a weathered wooden railing than ever live in the same space with you again."

"Wow." I mulled this over. "Really, just, *wow*. I don't think anyone has ever hated me this much."

"Well, for him I think it's more like loathing, if that makes sense."

"Yeah, yeah. I guess I can see that . . ."

"But look, man. I'll pray for you. I really will."

This took me aback. I'd heard through mutual friends that Luke had suddenly started attending church, had been baptized, but I wasn't too concerned about any of this. I was used to Luke's phases, and this seemed like a natural reaction to a drug-induced psychosis. It was actually a common enough story to not even really be that interesting.

Except that it was one of my dearest friends, a certified fucking atheist, and he was telling me that he was going *to pray for me.*

"Luke, what the fuck is wrong with you?"

"There's nothing wrong with me, Kevin. I've discovered a joy more wonderful than anything I've ever known. I've felt the presence of the Holy Spirit."

"What you felt was the toxins from some exceptionally potent mushrooms."

"No, Kevin, no. You don't understand. I've felt the love of Christ."

"Well, didn't Jesus have a parable about being a Good Samaritan? Taking in a stranger in need?"

"You have a home to go to, Kevin. And you weren't robbed. You fucked things up on your own, and now you've got to fix it. You know, the Lord helps those who help—"

"Bull fucking shit, motherfucker. Don't quote Ben Franklin to me. That's not even a Christian tenet you're expressing; that's directly in conflict with Christ's teachings."

"Good luck, Kevin." He hung up the phone.

So there really wasn't a soft place to lay my head besides the backseat of my car or a cozy bed in my parents' basement. I started walking to my car, but as I crossed the street I cut down the embankment to the flow of water from which the campground takes its name.

The spring is covered by a small brick structure, but there's room enough for several people to step in. There's a light submerged in the water, illuminating the natural rock cistern. There is enough room, if one feels so inclined, to submerge your whole body in the water.

I dipped my hands into the water and splashed some on my face. It was wonderfully cold and smelled of earth and moss. I plunged my hands in again and lifted them to my mouth and took a drink—at that moment, I could not imagine anything more perfect and pure than that cold water drawn directly from the ground. I was suddenly more thirsty than I could remember being in a long time, and I lay on my belly and pressed my face into the pool, gulping the water down. When I was finished, I leaned back against the wall, my face and shirt soaked, and I thought that maybe tomorrow I would call Lilith and ask her out for a cup of coffee. Maybe I'd look for a job as well.

Ecclesiasticus of Clyde

I was walking home after work in early November. It was still warm—the leaves were just finally beginning to dim and drift from the trees. I'd gotten a job at a business college that was total gravy—I taught basic grammar to would-be secretaries. It paid well, and so I was able to move into an apartment on Clement Avenue, just a few blocks from the school. I'd purchased an iPod with some of the blood money I received from the college, and I was contentedly floating through the world. Coltrane sounded so sweet and clear, as though I were at Birdland bopping with him.

I usually went in through the back entrance of my building. It was a more pleasing route with a courtyard of houses that reminded me slightly of Jimmy Stewart's view in *Rear Window*. I noticed my mother sitting in her white Lincoln Town Car. I removed my headphones and paused at the bottom of the steps as she got out of the car. She was sweating profusely.

"Where are my fucking paints? I know you stole them from the house."

"What?" I knew what she was talking about; she had an acrylic paint set that she wasn't using, and I'd asked her if I could have it. She'd said no, but I took it anyway because it had lingered untouched in her basement for over a year. My mother only descended into the basement to do laundry or to go to the garage; I knew the paints were fated the same as the various pieces of exercise equipment. Because her mental state was precarious, my mother spent most of her time sleeping or prowling the pantry. Occasionally a burst of energy would overtake her and she'd stir something up for a week or two, or volunteer at the church, but nothing really held her attention for any length of time. I genuinely wonder what the hell happened to my mother. She played college basketball, for Christ's sake! She read books, *good* books, and she'd been young and beautiful, and she went out and did things, and then somewhere along the way she just fell to pieces. That's half my DNA—and at this point I feel as though it's the half that's called most of the shots, and that being the case I feel nothing but a bleak future is in store for me. There must have been a point when she felt the nuttiness encroaching upon her—have I been at that point? I feel I'm there constantly, the splintered wooden door of sanity barred against the constant barrage of my other self, that obsessive, cynical leader of doubt who's constantly shouting, *Just give in! He wins in the end! We all know that Alamo shit isn't really noble when you add it up!* It's a sound I hear often on the precipice of sleep, when my heart will start to gallop as if trying to outrun that phantom sound of the lathe and the blade.

How long then before something as simple as missing acrylic paints sends me into an episode of compulsive aggression?

"You know what I'm talking about, you little shit. You

stole my paints and I'm not leaving until I get them back."
She was shaking and nearly shouting.

"Well, let's go upstairs. I think I have them up there." I
didn't have them up there, of course. I'd used them when I
took them nearly nine months ago. I was looking for a
stalling tactic; I figured I could call my dad and put her on
the phone with him. He was usually pretty good at getting
her to behave rationally. My mother trusted his motives.

As soon as we were in the apartment she started yelling,
"Where are my fucking paints? I'm getting tired of you
stealing my things!"

"What of yours have I stolen?"

"I don't keep a fucking list, asshole."

"I feel that you might."

She opened my refrigerator. "I'm taking one of your
Cokes."

"That's fine. Help yourself. Let me see where I put those
paints."

I walked back to my bedroom and went through the mo-
tions of examining the contents of my closet. I heard her
walk into the room I used as my office and begin rooting
through the other closet (my apartment only had two, plus
the pantry).

"So," I yelled to her, "are you finally going to do some
painting?"

"What business is it of yours?"

I walked into the other room and found her going
through my desk drawers.

"Well, you seem awful hot to get these paints back.
Also, I wouldn't keep them in my desk."

"I know that. I'm looking for the rest of my stuff."

"What stuff?"

"Don't fucking lie to me. I'm your mother, you little shit." She was wagging her finger in my face.

"Your paints might be in the pantry. I keep some other paints in there." She walked past me and headed toward the kitchen. I picked up the phone and dialed the folks' house. My brother answered.

"Hey, man, was Mom acting weird this morning?"

"She at your house?" He yawned.

"Yeah. She's acting wack, dude. I can't tell if she's had too much medication or not enough."

"She's been going on about those paints for days. I don't think she's really been sleeping. She's nuts."

I hung up with my brother and called my dad at work. This was serious business if my mother wasn't sleeping— she could easily be awake for five days at a time when one of these episodes settled on her. If you've ever stayed awake for two days, then you know all too well the way the world begins to melt into dreams; at five days, forget it—the brain is in a state of psychosis.

When my dad picked up his extension, I skipped the pleasantries and laid out the situation:

"Dad, Mom's at my place acting loopy."

He sighed. I heard the extension in the kitchen pick up; my mom's voice came on the line.

"Who is this?" she demanded.

"Amanda—," my dad began.

She cut him off. "David, don't you believe a fucking word he says. He stole those paints. He's a thief and I'm getting them back." She started to say something else, but I put down the phone I was listening on and walked into the kitchen to unplug her extension. My phone in the kitchen was an ancient rotary model that dated back to a time when the telephone company still issued customers a phone. The heavy, harvest gold model was weighted so that it doubled as a blunt object with which to kill intruders or philandering spouses. It was not, however, well suited for flight, which worked to my advantage that afternoon, otherwise I might not be here to impose my meandering tale upon you, devoted reader. As soon as I'd turned my back from unplugging the phone from the wall in the kitchen, I made it perhaps five paces when I felt what seemed like a concrete block hit me square in the back. I dropped to the floor instantly, the wind knocked out of me. The phone clattered to the floor at the same time, the bell inside it's sturdy casing clanging in such a way as to give voice to how my brain felt; I realized she'd been aiming for my head, and I was a lucky bastard that the telephone was not meant to defy gravity. I was down for a few minutes while my mom stood over me ranting.

"That's right, you little son of a bitch, you thief. I'll teach you to steal from me. Now where's my goddamned paints? And my brushes? What's wrong? Cat got your tongue? You sold them didn't you, or gave them to one of your little whores? I'm going to call them and find out. I'll get their phone numbers—you can't hide anything from me."

I believed her. Many of my experiences with my mother had been an exercise in the techniques of interrogation and covert surveillance. I do not wish to catalog the humiliations I've suffered in my life because of her intrusions, but I will extend this small item for your consideration: A few days after I was dismissed from my position at the art school, my mother called the human resources director and asked him to give me my job back. I've no idea what she said, nor do I wish to know. Imagine how you would feel, sympathetic reader, if at the age of twenty-nine, after enduring a very public firing, your mother called your former place of employment just to see if they wouldn't give you one more chance?

And that's just the tip of the iceberg, friends. Now she was in my apartment, bludgeoning me with kitsch, and taunting me with the promise of more humiliation in the future. I got my breath back and slowly got up from the floor. I kept reminding myself that I was not dealing with someone in her rational mind.

"Mom, you need to leave my house."

"I'm not going anywhere until I get my paints back."

"Then I'm calling the police."

She began to laugh. "Oh, I'd like to see you call the police. I'll tell them you've got drugs in the house."

"I don't have drugs in the house." I started back into my bedroom to retrieve the phone. I had no intention of calling the police, even as pissed as I was. Those guys have tough, thankless jobs, and I appreciate what they do—I certainly couldn't do it, but I'm secure in the knowledge that I have a big dick, so I don't feel the need to get a job where I'm licensed to be an asshole. The police are a last resort, and only then if you're dealing with strangers. You don't call the police on family or friends. That's just fucking un-American. Also, I had drugs in the house.

I stood in my bedroom for a moment. I didn't know what to do. I wasn't going to leave, because who knew what havoc my mother would bring to my apartment. Granted, I didn't have much she could damage besides books and cats, but the cats had already been driven into seclusion by the telephone exchange. I walked back out into the living room and tried on my best authoritarian tone:

"You will leave my apartment now, or I will physically throw you out." My voice was quivering.

"Try it, you pussy."

I grabbed her by the arm and started for the door; she didn't budge. I grabbed her arm with both my hands and pulled—she still didn't move. My mother outweighed me by a good seventy-five pounds then, but she was also fifty-four years old with a heart condition and chronic pain. I couldn't figure out how she was rooted to the floor. But she'd begun to huff—this wasn't entirely easy for her.

I let go of her and began to walk back to my bedroom again.

"I told you that you couldn't do it. You pussy. You can't—"

I wheeled around and lunged at her with both of my arms up as though I were blocking a tackle. At least I think that's how it looked—I'm not really sure; I don't watch football. I caught her off guard and she went stumbling back against the wall. She tried to slap me but I caught her hand and drew my fist back.

"Do it! You just fucking do it! I dare you!"

I slammed my fist as hard as I could into the wall next to her head; she didn't even blink. Then she kneed me square in the balls.

I didn't hit the floor again, but it was close. I stumbled, I grabbed my crotch, I felt the nausea begin that so often accompanies a solid ball-racking. I suppose my mother felt she'd exhausted her purpose in tormenting me, and she quickly retreated into the kitchen and out the back door and down the steps. I managed to make it to the top of the landing as she was opening her car door.

"This is it!" I yelled. "We're done! You're dead to me!" It seems completely stupid in retrospect—what a B-grade, faggy exhortation. But what else could I have yelled?

My mother looked at me coolly, then flipped me the bird—*with both hands*—then got in her car and drove away. I went back into my apartment, made sure all the doors were locked, then went into the bathroom and took a steaming, muddy crap—my typical reaction to extreme emotional duress—and I cried tears that matched the heat of my bowel movement. I really and truly hated my mother, and I felt terrible about it.

When I finally lifted myself from the toilet, I attacked the bong with professional zeal and sat in my apartment as it grew dark and watched as the cats emerged from their hiding places. They looked wary, but in only a few minutes they were comfortable enough to each piss on my doormat.

My dad called around six and tried to square the afternoon with me.

"Kevin, look, you know how your mother gets. It's really not her—it's the disease."

"The disease threw a fucking telephone at me, man! She was aiming for my head! I'm just lucky she sucks. But look, Dad, this is it. I've had it. I'm done speaking to her."

"She's not just your mother; she's my wife."

"Stand by your wife; it's what you have to do. But what I have to do is extricate myself from that madness, and if that means cutting you out, well, it's nothing personal; it's just the way it has to be for me to feel healthy."

"You'll get over it."

"I'll see you down the line," I said, and hung up the phone.

I kept in touch with my brother; I couldn't abandon him to that lunacy, no matter what our differences. Besides, he and I were getting along better than ever. However, my brother was the only family member exempt from my code of silence. Even though it was my mother whom I ultimately wanted to punish, I had to break ties with everyone: grandparents, aunts, uncles—the whole shooting match. I can't provide an adequate explanation for why I felt this way, except that it seemed I was never going to find the thrill of myself under the oppressive yoke of my family. I was tired of feeling that I owed them something, or that they had some claim on my time.

And so it came to pass that I was alone on Christmas Eve.

Lilith invited me over to her family's house, but I skipped out on that nightmare. I felt my own dysfunctional clan had given me enough on-the-job training with fucked-up family dynamics so that I could spot their unstable behavior in my sleep.

My friend James had also offered to have me come over to his house and hang out with his family. His wife had moved out three days before and was living in an apartment around the block. She was coming over so that Christmas wouldn't be too screwy for their four-year-old. I begged off that one for all the obvious reasons.

In an odd way, it seemed people couldn't stand the idea of someone being free from the shackles of family on a major holiday. I was fairly certain that an opportunity such as a solitary Christmas would come my way only once, so I bought a rotisserie chicken for the cats at the grocery store and some sugar cookies and vegetarian baked beans for myself and spent the evening watching *It's a Wonderful Life* as the cats tore the bird apart.

When spring came, it seemed as though I were living on a little corner of paradise in the city: the people who lived next to the apartment maintained a ridiculously beautiful garden and small patch of green lawn that thrived in the shade of aged oaks and a towering magnolia tree. The people across the street who were perpetually restoring their house had a yard of tropical flowers and daughters in full bloom. It was a glorious place to be. And it wasn't even yet April.

I couldn't keep myself out of the sunshine. My contract with the business college had concluded, without incident, in February, and I'd picked up a few night classes at the community college. Since the return of the warm weather I'd been spending the afternoons on the front lawn, lazily scribbling halfhearted poems in my journal. Occasionally I'd string together some words that I thought weren't too bad, but it didn't seem the same as it once did.

On one of these balmy, late-March days as I loafed under an oak, I saw a white Lincoln Town Car slowly cruising down my street. I watched as it came to a stop in front of my apartment complex, and I thought, *That's weird. What are the odds of a car like the one my parents have showing up in front of my apartment?* When my mother and father both emerged, I almost went straight into a panic attack.

In the five months since my mother had come to my apartment and accosted me, I'd more or less managed to avoid all contact with her. She continued to call, but since I had caller ID, I could screen her out. In a few instances I'd answered the phone without checking, but when I heard her voice, I politely said, "I'm not speaking with you. I'm hanging up now," and that was the end of that.

Now here she was, and with my father in tow. If I'd been inside my apartment, I could at least have pretended not to be home, but they'd caught me scribbling belabored verse right out in the open.

I stood up as they walked across the yard and said, "Hey. What's happening?" And then as an afterthought: "No one died, did they?"

"No," my dad said. "Everyone's fine."

"Good," I said. "Good." We stood there just staring at one another.

"Nice day to be outside," my dad said.

I looked around as though it had just dawned on me that I was, in fact, outdoors. "Yeah, I suppose it is. Days like this make you wish you had a convertible."

"Yeah, that would be nice." We hit another dead end in the conversation.

After a moment I said, "So, you guys want to come up-stairs?"

"Sure," my dad said.

We filed up the stairs in silence, and once we were inside my apartment, we sat down around the table.

"Can I get you something to drink?" I asked.

"No," my dad said. "I'm fine. Amanda?" My mother shook her head; since she'd gotten out of the car, she hadn't said a word, and it looked as though tears were trembling on the edge of her lower eyelids.

"Okay then. So what brings y'all by here?"

"Well, we kind of figured—"

"I'm sorry, Kevin!" And my mom began to sob and buried her face in her hands. She said something else, but it was completely inaudible through her hands and her gulps for air.

My dad rolled his eyes. "Well, there you have it. Your mother is sorry. I don't know what went on, but she's sorry, and we miss you, and it just seemed like if we didn't come down here, then we weren't ever going to see you again."

I nodded my head but didn't reply.

"And you know your grandmother is in bad shape, and your grandfather isn't getting any younger either, and they miss you, too. Also, with Brandon moving to Arizona . . ." He trailed off as my mother's sobs became more hysterical.

I was already clued into the news that Brandon was heading West. He'd stumbled across a Web site soliciting seasonal workers for the Grand Canyon's North Rim. I don't know where he got the notion to apply, but I guess when you've lived in the same place for a quarter of a century, you just wake up one morning and decide you've had enough.

"This is all well and good," I said, "but I'm not about to join the circus again where you guys are concerned unless I can be certain that she"—I pointed a hostile finger at my mother—"isn't going to flip out and attack me and belittle me ever again. I've had all the crazy I can handle in one life, and I've got my own problems. I can't be the target for someone else's delusions."

"There won't be any more of that," my dad said. Then

he turned to my mom and said, "Is there going to be any more nonsense, Amanda?"

She took her hands from her face, removing her glasses as she did so, and wiped her eyes ever so dramatically with a tissue, then with a faltering voice said, "No, there . . . won't be . . . ever again."

"Well, good enough for me," I said. "You guys want to go get a slice of pizza?"

In the months before my brother departed he'd been helping my grandfather out. Essentially he was doing a little cooking and cleaning, which let my grandfather devote his full attention to his ailing wife. When my brother left, I volunteered to help out. My motives weren't entirely altruistic—after all, I still owed my grandfather money from when he'd bailed me out with that weed dealer. In my mind, I didn't just owe him the cash; my debt was far greater, because you don't stiff family members when they've saved your ass. My time away from my family had at least offered me an interesting vantage point from which to ponder the nature of what family meant.

I was accustomed to walking straight into my grandparents' house without knocking. However, the first day I showed up to lend a hand, I found the front door to my grandfather's house bolted solidly. I rang the bell, and after a few minutes I heard the jangle of his keys on the other side of the door, then the turn of the lock, then another lock, and then the door opened, after which he unlocked and opened the storm door. I looked at him curiously.

"Hey, Kevin."

"What's with the locked doors, Papaw?"

"Safety." He didn't offer further explanation, and I didn't need any. I knew he wasn't worried about marauders and rapists; his security precautions were designed to keep my grandmother inside.

It was only eleven in the morning, but they were already sitting in the kitchen eating lunch; my grandfather was working on a pimento-cheese sandwich, and my grandmother had a bowl of oatmeal, and it was absolutely depressing to see her. She'd been in the wheelchair the last time I'd been to their house some seven or eight months ago, but she was otherwise just a woman in a wheelchair flirting with senility. In the time I'd gone AWOL from the lives of the Kecks, my grandmother had basically become an aged infant.

She was seated in her wheelchair before her bowl of oatmeal, lazily spooning at the contents. Most of it made it into her mouth, but a great deal landed on her bib. Her hair was unkempt, and she was in a frumpy housedress. In her prime, while not the most stylish woman, she took great pride in looking and dressing smartly.

My grandfather sat back down at the head of the table and picked up his sandwich, then looked at me. "Are you hungry? You want something to eat?"

"No, I'm fine."

"Well, have a seat and talk to us. We haven't seen you in so long. Are you still teaching?"

"Yeah, not as much. Just in the evenings."

"Do you like where you are?"

"No. I like teaching, but I don't like where I'm teaching. It's just . . ." I trailed off. I couldn't imagine that anything I was saying was remotely interesting. I'd found out later that anything I had to say to my grandfather was interesting. He spent nearly all day, every day, trapped with a woman in an alternate reality. Any conversation, however mundane, was a welcome reprieve.

"Dewey!" my grandmother yelled. "When did you get here?"

I smiled at her; I didn't know what to say. My grandfather slowly chewed his sandwich, and when he'd swallowed, he said, "Mom, that's not Dewey. Dewey's dead. He's been dead a long time. That's Kevin, David's boy. Your oldest grandchild."

"Well, I didn't recognize you without my glasses." She was, in fact, wearing her glasses.

"It's okay, Mamaw," I said. "Sometimes I don't even recognize myself." She smiled a blissful, thoughtless smile at me.

"You're a good-looking fella, ain't ya?" She didn't say it as a grandmother doting on her grandson's handsomeness, but rather with a comely tone I'd never heard come out of her mouth before.

I stood up from the table quickly. "Well, Papaw, what do you need me to do?"

"Well, the whole house really needs cleaning. Just pick a spot and go."

While I hate to admit this, that's exactly the words I wanted to hear. Long before I'd taken my compulsive cleaning to the extreme, I was just a well-balanced obsessive neat freak. I like things in their proper place. I hate dust. I don't mind mopping or vacuuming. Butlers are my favorite characters in novels, and I adore a woman in a maid outfit. When staying at a hotel I try to avoid the corridors in the mornings, lest a housekeeping lass prove tempting with her feather duster and latex gloves.

And so I set myself to the task of cleaning their house. I did what any sensible person would do regarding vacuuming and dusting, but I also attacked the ceiling fans, the blinds, and the slats on the intake vent for the central air.

The roughest part of my labors, however, was the bathroom. I cleaned crap from places on the toilet that defied the laws of physics. I daresay that the "splatter effect" was absolutely supernatural. The sad fact was that no matter how efficiently I cleaned the bathroom, whenever I returned the following day, or the day after that, it was as if I'd never stepped foot in there.

Besides cleaning, my other purpose was to sit with my grandmother and give my grandfather some relief from his endless toils. During those hours while I sat and watched television with her, my grandfather either retreated to the basement to work on the lawn mower—years later he was still trying to resurrect it—or he took to his new John Deere and mowed the sprawling lawn that had been in my charge as a teenager. I realized during those first few weeks that he didn't need time to rest, he needed time to do something different. Looking after my grandmother was exhausting—and I was just thirty-one. He was eighty-four, and his athletic frame that had once swaggered, even in senior years, had shrunk to a thinness that rivaled my own lithe, puny body.

My grandmother had to be lifted out of her bed in the morning and helped to the bathroom; then she had to be dressed and placed in her wheelchair; then she had to be fed. Often this was followed by another trip to the bathroom,

which was at the opposite end of the house from the kitchen.
If you didn't get her wheeled back there in time, *watch out.*

Every day after lunch my grandmother took a nap. Everyone looked forward to her naps, because it was a reprieve
for all involved. She was helped into these naps by a small,
green pill. I assumed these pills were for blood pressure or
arthritis. After a few weeks my grandfather trusted me
enough to put me in charge of administering my grandmother's medicine, and when I had time to examine her pills
more closely, I realized they were one-milligram Klonopins:
essentially Valium, but more effective in the treatment of
anxiety. Also they knocked you the fuck out. I read the in-
structions on the bottle; my grandmother was supposed to
be taking four a day. I assumed the script was written as
such so that there would never be an emergency situation,
but my grandfather, child of the Great Depression, was ever
frugal—at most I saw my grandmother take two a day: one
for her afternoon nap, and then one as the sun went down.
It was pretty stressful helping to take care of her, so when I
administered her pill in the afternoons I prescribed one for
myself as well and spent the next few hours cleaning in a
state more blissful than I'd ever known. Add a little marijuana to that and I had a recipe for eternal happiness.

I'd like to confess that I was doing this because it was
brutally hard to watch my grandmother in her current condition, but I believe it has become rather evident to the
reader at this point that I just happen to like drugs. Before
I used drugs recreationally, I spent most of my time en-
tombed in my room, the windows covered with tinfoil, letting the dreaming darkness harbor my reality.

And this new little twist of the tranquilizer . . . it took

away the acute panic that sometimes accompanied an intense buzz. Philistines are under the impression that all marijuana simply makes you not care. On the contrary, it often amplifies your cares just a bit too much, and the spaghetti sauce you dribbled on the rug the evening before suddenly becomes as vexing as Lady Macbeth's spot.

Besides, under the influence of the tranquilizers, it was easy to have a conversation with my grandmother. The continental drift of her memory was a ride that you could actually enjoy, because her sense of the past was more vivid than it would ever have been had she actually tried to recall it in her more lucid years.

"Tell me about you and Papaw getting married," I asked her one afternoon.

She looked up from the magazine she was reading; you could hand her a magazine and she'd read it cover to cover, often out loud. The Alzheimer's had actually made her a more voracious reader than she'd ever been, and she never had trouble recognizing a single word, though she retained absolutely nothing about what she'd read even seconds after finishing a sentence. Put a pen in her hand and ask her to write her name, and she would stare at the pen and paper as though she'd never seen such things before.

"Come on," I said. "Didn't you and Papaw slip off to get married?"

"Yeah," she said, smiling.

"And then what?"

"What?"

"What happened when you two slipped off?"

"We got married."

"Yes, but how?"

"What do you mean, how? Are you stupid?" she hissed. The Alzheimer's had given her a temper, and it flared for the worse when she was frustrated.

Only by chance did anyone know the circumstances of my grandparents' marriage. During one Christmas dinner at my uncle John's house I asked my grandmother if she remembered the first time she'd ever seen my grandfather.

"Of course I do," she said. "He came walking into the part of Brookford Mill where I worked; he was a loom fixer, and I worked picking out the bad spots on the weaves of cloth that came out of the loom. He had this jet-black hair and blue eyes, and he just looked like a movie star."

I looked across the table to where my grandfather was sitting; he was staring at his plate, chewing his food, trying not to smile.

"Papaw," I said. "Do you remember when you first saw Mamaw?"

"Well, there were a lot of girls that worked in that mill. But I reckon I noticed her right pretty quick when it counted."

"So did you two date long before you got married?"

"Not too long," my grandfather said.

"Did you have a ceremony?"

My grandmother and grandfather exchanged a glance; I saw him smile at her.

"We eloped," my grandmother said. This caught the attention of everyone at the table, and suddenly we were all demanding to hear the story. "Well, we told our folks we were going over to Statesville on Saturday to see a movie, and when we got there, we went into the movie, watched the first little bit, and then we went to the justice of the peace to get married. Now Clyde was only seventeen, and I was nineteen, but because we didn't have any identification, that justice of the peace gave me a real hard time as to whether or not I was actually nineteen. But he finally married us, and then we went back to the movie to see how it ended. You know, just in case anyone asked." Then she picked up her fork and went back to eating, as though she'd just given us an account of something as mundane as the weather. My dad and his brother and sister looked positively stunned. For some reason no one had ever bothered to tell them this story.

My grandmother was content to conclude the story there, it seemed, but my aunt Susie said, "Christ, Margaret—there has to be more to it. What happened when you got back to Hickory?"

My grandfather cut in, "I dropped her off at her mom's house and I went back to mine."

"And that was that?" I asked.

"Well, no." My grandmother actually sounded a little irritated about a fact that was over sixty years old. "That Monday at the mill . . . what was that guy's name, Clyde? Well, I can't remember . . . it was Bill something or other . . . he took the paper from Statesville, and of course it listed all the marriages, and so he'd told everyone at the mill by the time Clyde and I got to work."

"And then what?"

"I took her home with me that night," my grandfather said.

I spent a lot of afternoons telling that story to my

grandmother over and over again, hoping that something might stir within her memory, but it was gone completely.

My grandfather was out mowing the grass one afternoon in early July, and my grandmother was asleep in her recliner where she took all of her afternoon naps. I'd run out of basic things to clean, so I was using a Q-tip to remove years of dust from around the various buttons and crevices of all the electronic equipment in the house. Suddenly my grandmother yelled, "Clyde! Clyde!"

I walked over and knelt beside her. "Papaw's outside, Mamaw. What is it?"

"I need to go to the bathroom."

"Well, hang on a second and let me get him."

"I've got to go now, Dewey. Help me up."

This wasn't in my job description.

I got in front of her, lifted her out of the recliner and into her wheelchair. Since she'd become less mobile, her weight had bloomed toward two hundred pounds. I can lift two hundred pounds on a barbell, but a two-hundred-pound woman, dopey from Klonopin, was another matter.

As I was pushing her down the hallway, she said, "Hurry, Dewey. Hurry. I ain't gonna make it. Oh, Dad's gonna be so mad at me. Don't let me mess, Dewey."

It was absolutely heart-wrenching. She had no idea who I was, and she was afraid of upsetting her father, who'd been dead for sixty years.

I worked the wheelchair down the hallway with all the precision of Luke Skywalker making his descent on the

Death Star. We made it to the bathroom, I lifted her out of her wheelchair, but, alas, friends, the force was not with me. While I consider myself rather adept at wriggling young ladies out of their clothes, I had absolutely no practice when it came to older women.

As soon as she was upright, my grandmother began to sway on her unsteady feet as I worked furiously to raise her housedress and then—ah, Jesus, how there are some things you wish you could forget—lower her adult diapers and get her on the toilet. No dice. Just as I was about to lower her Depends, my sweet little grandmother who had been as much of a mother to me as my own mother, but better because she wasn't so loony, ripped a wet blast that echoed as a thunderclap in the bathroom, and the brown sludge began to drip out of her diapers and down her legs. Tears filled her eyes, and she went limp in my arms, and as I was standing at an awkward angle I had no choice but to lower her slowly to the floor.

She began to scream, an awful piercing shriek that was painful in the enclosed space of the bathroom. And the smell? I've rarely felt so helpless as I did then, with my grandmother so vulnerable and terrified. I closed my eyes and proceeded to get a grip. If I could shovel and sift for cat turds daily at my apartment, surely I could help my wailing grandmother.

I grabbed her by her arms and raised her to a sitting position. Pressing my face to hers, I felt her hot tears against my cheek and struggled to keep my own at bay. She had stopped screaming, and when I felt I had it together, I pulled back and looked her in the eye.

"Mamaw, you took care of me when I couldn't take care of myself, and now I'm going to take care of you. So I don't want you to be afraid, because there's nothing to worry about. I'm here. Everything is going to be all right."

"Okay, Dewey."

"Okay," and with that I placed my arms beneath hers and lifted her from the floor and into the shower. I took off her dress and shoes and socks, and the adult diaper, and I bathed her. I didn't enjoy a single moment of it—washing an eighty-six-year-old woman caked in shit is about as thrilling as it sounds. I don't recall what I said to her. I think I mused on the irony of our situation; I tried to make her laugh. I thought some lucid part of her, buried in the maze of shifting memory, might be vaguely aware and ashamed that her oldest grandson was seeing her in this condition and taking care of her. But if there was a glimmer of awareness, I didn't catch it.

My grandfather came into the bedroom as I was dressing her. He looked mortified and puzzled all at once. I quickly explained what had happened, and he nodded and listened, and when I was done, he crossed the room to where I was and put his hand on my shoulder. He looked in my eyes, but said nothing, and then we finished dressing her together.

I've been hunting a few times in my life. A lot of the friends I grew up with took great pride in the first deer they killed, even the first possum—and killing a possum is about as difficult as opening a can of Pepsi. But without fail they all expressed the same sensation of *becoming a man* when they killed an animal. But if anything, I felt like less of a man when I killed, as though by taking something out of the world forever I was taking something out of myself.

This sense of being a man has vexed me most of my life.

I'm not prone to fighting or violence (unless we're talking spankings), and I've never excelled at sports. But that day I felt I was called upon to be a man in a way I could never have anticipated. It was a passage of compassion.

I was using the Q-tips to clean again, but this time I was working my way around the oversize, neon buttons on the telephone in my grandparents' kitchen. For some reason, whenever I clean a phone it rings; I keep expecting a genie to be on the other end, but it never works out that way.

"What?"

"Uh, Mr. Keck?" It was a woman's voice.

"Well, yes, but you have three Mr. Kecks to choose from. Which one were you looking for?"

"Clyde Keck?"

"He's out mowing the grass." Always with the grass . . .

"Is this the son who came with him to the hospital yesterday?"

"No, that would be my father, David. This is his grandson Kevin."

"Is your father there? Or is there a number where I could reach him?"

I gave her the number for my folks' place next door, and I hung up the phone. My dad had driven my grandfather to the VA hospital the previous day for his annual checkup.

When my grandfather came in from mowing the grass an hour later, he'd barely sat down when my dad came grimly through the door and asked if they could speak privately. They disappeared into the room that functioned as my grandfather's office. I stood around the corner and listened as best I could. I didn't hear everything, but I heard enough: chest X-ray, lesion, cancer. I looked at my grandmother sleeping in her recliner. The family had discussed—out of my grandfather's presence, of course—what might happen if he should die before my grandmother. No one wanted to face that prospect. Things were tough as it was without a professional nurse to take care of my grandmother, and my grandfather flat out refused to consign her to an assisted-living facility. He'd grown up in a time when the old folks' home was just a step above a death camp. This was his wife of sixty-seven years. I suppose when you've put in that kind of time, you don't just bail on someone.

I started to dust the candy dishes. They were devoid of any treats, but my grandmother liked having them around. When my grandfather and my father emerged from the hall into the living room, my dad looked pale. My grandfather, on the other hand, looked as though my dad had come by to tell him about a crabgrass problem.

After my dad had gone, my grandfather said, "Kevin, come with me."

He began to take me on a tour of the house. It took a few rooms for me to catch on—he was showing me the things that only he would know about. When the dryer wasn't working, here was the tool to adjust the heating element; here was the ointment when Mamaw's feet began to crack; if the central air didn't come on when the thermostat was adjusted, this was the fuse; a gun was hidden in a sock in this drawer, so be careful; extra batteries for the smoke detectors were at the top of the closet in the hallway; if there was ever a financial emergency, I should check Mamaw's old purses in the back of their closet; the socket set in the gray toolbox belonged to my great-great-grandfather on my grandmother's side; this was a tool that was used to repair looms; this was a cobbler's iron for molding shoes, but it worked better as a doorstop; this was the jewelry my grandmother liked best.

When I left that day, I knew he would not be taking any treatment. He didn't say anything about it, and I didn't ask.

Who knows how our deaths are chosen for us? My grandmother didn't deserve her slow, wilting fate, but from a distance it seems she was spared the one loss that would have ripped her heart apart. And my grandfather? If his impending departure grieved him in any way, I never saw it. On the first Monday in September he mowed his grass. I stood watching him from the front porch. When I was a child, I would ride on his lap on the lawn mower that now sat in the basement and which would never be fixed. When he came inside, he said to me he hoped it was the last time for the season that he had to mow; it was beginning to wear him out. On Tuesday, he said he felt a little foggy-headed, and he didn't bother to shave.

We were all there on Wednesday. My grandfather had been unconscious most of the morning, and his bed had been pushed up against the window. My uncle was sitting at his bedside when he sat up and began to reach for the blinds as though trying to open them. My uncle did it for him, letting in the last brilliant rays of sun. My uncle said, "Dad, do you want to play some cards?"

My grandfather said, "Yes." And then he was dead.

Benedictines

When I started college at a school that was built by Benedictine monks in the nineteenth century, it was my intention to become a priest. I'm not exactly sure what my motivation was; I was not raised Catholic. My family was of lapsed-Presbyterian heritage—which is a way of talking around the issue that we became Methodists because the services were shorter and this was of singular importance to my father during football season. Also, I did not grow up in an area that was home to many people who were Catholic. If anything, my hometown lived up to the South's lingering anti-Catholic sentiments, a feeling steeped in the traditions of evangelical Protestantism.

But I had dreams. Literal dreams in which I heard the voice of God speaking to me and urging me down a path of servitude and faith. The dreams were not frequent—perhaps three in two years—but they were not the mind's distorted impressions of daily junk. They bordered more on what I thought were visions; I felt unsettled after waking from each of them, as though in the night I'd somehow traveled outside my body.

In one dream I am standing at the back of a church sanctuary. It appears as though everyone is taking Communion, but when I look more closely, I realize everyone is having some variation of sexual contact with a piece of fruit. As soon as I realize what's going on, I shout something to the effect of "I don't think this is what Jesus intended!" The congregants cease their activities with the fruit and with cries of "Nonbeliever!" begin hurling the objects of their affections at me. I end up on my knees, drenched in fruit pulp, and I clearly remember staring at a mango and thinking, *How to heal this mango?*

There was no direct line of communication with God in that dream, no clear message as to what it all meant and what I should do. And to some extent, that I let a dream of this sort inform my decision making places me in a suspect category when it comes to judging my sanity. Had I consulted with my peers regarding these dreams, I've no doubt the mockery would have been of a severity usually reserved for practitioners of bestiality.

Instead, I sought the counsel of the minister of our church, who actually treated the dreams as mystical revelations. Our minister, Pastor Benny, had come to the pulpit from the meat counter—he'd worked as a butcher for twenty-five years before receiving the call. It doesn't seem surprising at all in retrospect that a man who "got the call" from God while cleaving carcasses should see my story of fruit fucking as sane.

Pastor Benny urged me to follow the path that God had placed before me. He didn't venture to tell me what he thought that path might be. I settled on attending college thirty minutes away from home, at a small Catholic school that didn't require Algebra II. And which fed my fantasy

of being guided by God toward a destiny of spiritual fulfillment.

Plus it was cool to tell people you were becoming a
priest, especially if you had a beer in your hand. Oh, those
numerous parties where I clung piously to the keg, eyeing
the tan legs and pert breasts that would ultimately be forbidden to me!

That was half the charm, of course, in becoming a
man of the cloth for the Catholic team: romantic martyr-
dom. I'd already wandered into that lonely-hearted trap
unintentionally—as a teenager my luck with the ladies
was so abysmal that when I was sixteen, I considered for
a few weeks whether I might be gay—so why not just
take it to the next level? At least there was the possibility
that some girl might take pity on my future of celibacy
and give me one last glimpse of heaven on earth. As it
turned out, teenage girls were not nearly as aroused at
the prospect of bedding a would-be priest as I imagined.
They were actually quite freaked out.

Once I was at college, however, and that romantic fantasy
began to manifest itself in real terms, I wasn't so sure about
the role I'd been playing. If I wasn't reminded about my supposed "purpose" by the various crucifixes and statues of
saints that littered the campus, I was certainly made aware
by the monks' constant presence. The abbey was at the center of the campus, and most of the older buildings had been
built with bricks made by the monks. The brothers moved
about the grounds quietly in their black robes, often appearing out of nowhere and smiling like cheerful reapers.

I made few friends in those first few days and weeks.

When I was tired of reading or studying, I would go for long walks around the campus late at night. More often than not I ended up in the shadows of the trees on the quad, curious to see if any of the females who lived on the top floors of the dorm had neglected to lower their blinds.

On one of these walks I found myself down at a grotto that was carved into the side of a hill at the base of the monastery. The grotto had a shrine for the Holy Mother. The previous spring, when I'd gone on the tour for prospective students, the admissions counselor who led the tour told how the grotto and shrine were built by a monk who'd been gravely ill, but after praying to the Virgin Mary he'd miraculously gotten well, and this was his way of showing thanks. Praying to Jesus, praying to God—the odds always seemed fifty-fifty. But all the stories I heard of the Holy Mother ended with absolute results. I needed results.

It struck me as idiotic that I should kneel in the dark before a statue (it wasn't completely dark—the Virgin was cast in a subtle glow by an artfully arranged floodlight) of someone who is revered in part because she never had sex. In all truth I should have been kneeling before Dionysus or Pan, but after I'd made absolutely certain that no one was around to see me, I went down on my knees, bowed my head, and rattled off a list of requests. I can't say that I felt all that transformed by the experience, but it had an air of importance that praying in bed lacked.

Thus, my nightly ritual became one of covert prayer. I would have been mortified had anyone known where I was going or witnessed my act of humility. I begged for guidance, and whenever I opened my eyes, the Holy Mother was always staring at me with a benevolent pity that seemed very much like that of Glinda the Good Witch of the North, as though I'd been toting the answers to my problems with me all along.

A month into the semester, two of the guys on my hall, Cody and Ken, decided after I'd played cards with them a few times that I was "cool enough" to be invited on what they referred to as "adventuring." They'd assumed from my music collection that I liked to get high. Normally, it would be the right guess for someone with a plethora of Grateful Dead and King Crimson albums. However, my background was more in beer. But that didn't cause me to hesitate when Cody and Ken poked their heads in my door one night and asked if I wanted to do some adventuring.

Even though it was only late September, Ken had a long overcoat on and was moving with the stiffness of the recently risen undead.

"What's with you?" I asked. Cody and Ken were walking with purpose, and I trailed behind them as a squeaky third wheel. Ken didn't say anything but instead flashed me his airline pilot's smile: Ken wanted to fly jets, and he had the archetypal good looks of a captain for Pan Am in an aging *Life* magazine ad.

I turned to say something to Cody, but he cut me off before the words were out: "Quit being so fucking anxious."

We walked beyond the dorms, past the tennis courts, across the soccer field, and into the line of trees on the opposite side. A series of steps hidden from view by drooping pines led up to a service road behind the field. We stopped midway up the steps, and Ken began unbuttoning his overcoat. He produced a three-foot-long, blue tube with a magician's flourish.

"Gentlemen, I give you Blue Boy."

"Sweet," Cody said, and took Blue Boy from Ken's hands and began to examine it.

"You smoke much, Keck?"

"Not really."

"Well, take it easy on Blue Boy. He'll put you on your ass."

Cody handed the bong back to Ken and took out his sack of weed. He packed the bowl full and Ken handed Blue Boy to me.

"What do I do?"

"There's a little hole on the back; that's the carb. Put your finger over that and I'll light the bowl while you suck through the tube. When you're ready to take a hit, let your finger off the carb and inhale. But seriously—go easy."

Prior to this, my only experience smoking pot occurred in eleventh grade during a party when a friend's older brother, T. J., managed to coax me into the garage to get high with him and his hot girlfriend. It was, of course, the girlfriend that tipped the scales of peer pressure. I remember clearly that her tube top made her breasts look as though they were more restrained than clothed. That night the smoking apparatus had been a radiator hose with a socket at the other end that functioned as the bowl. I took two hits, T. J. declared me "cooler than I thought you was, man," and I weaved my way back into the living room, where I promptly fell asleep behind the couch.

Ken flicked the lighter, and I saw his face and Cody's smiling at me with keen interest. I lifted the tube slowly to my mouth, and when I did, Ken put the flame to the weed and said, "Okay, suck." Cody began to snicker, and I thought I was going to as well, but then Ken was saying, "Let the carb off," and my lungs filled with smoke. I began to cough. "Hold it as long as you can, man," Cody was saying, and between coughs I heard the bong fire up again, and then once more. I was still coughing when the bong appeared in front of me again and Ken said, "Ready for another?"

I wasn't, but I took another hit anyway. And another. Ken remarked that Cody's weed was "primo"; Cody mentioned that it came from his cousin and that it was always around. I said nothing. I felt every woodland creature peering from its concealed, darkened space . . . watching us.

But other than a raspy throat and a slight light-headedness, I felt nothing. After Cody and Ken took a few more hits we walked back down the steps and toward the soccer field. No lights illuminated this part of campus, and for that reason it was especially popular for clandestine activities. A couple sprawled in the grass, limbs entwined. I looked up at the stars.

"Dudes," I said. "Check it."

The three of us stopped in the middle of the field. Cody and Ken looked up at the sky. Instead of appearing like pinholes poked in a blanket, the stars floated separately from the sky—everything had taken on a new depth.

"I think I can see the distance between the stars." I said that, but no one ever answered, and it's possible I just thought it. Then to make certain I said:

"I think I'm stoned."

"You should major in geology."

It was a stupid joke, but we all giggled and suddenly lost interest in the heavens. We began to walk back to the dorm.

Ken said, "But seriously. What are you guys majoring in?"

"Fuck if I know," Cody said.

I didn't answer and Ken elbowed me.

"Keck!"

"What?"

"You got a major?"

"Yeah. Religion."

"Religion?" Cody spit the word out. "What the fuck are you going to do with that?"

Something about the tone of his voice led me to believe that explaining my dream about the fruit would only invite pain.

"I don't know. I'd thought about, you know . . . the abbey."

Ken and Cody burst out laughing.

Cody started to wipe tears from his eyes, and a puff of smoke followed by a shadow emerged from the trees.

"Ah, the laughter of boys, it warms my heart to hear it." Father X—— was standing in front of us, the orange glow of his pipe smoldering in the dark like a watchful eye.

We all mumbled greetings to Father X——; he taught one of our humanities courses and was also one of the more accessible monks. The isolation of the Abbey gave most of the monks the demeanor of edgy postal employees. Father X—— looked and laughed exactly like Santa Claus, except his white beard was yellowed with nicotine around his mouth.

"What brings you boys out here tonight?"

"Stargazing," Cody said quickly.

Father X—— looked to the sky and extended his arm, pointing toward something indistinguishable with the stem of his pipe. He opened his mouth as if he were about to begin a lecture, but then returned the pipe to his mouth and winked at us.

"Very good, very good. Well, God bless." He brushed past us and started in the direction of the soccer field.

"Creepy," Cody said, and Ken and I voiced our agreement as we walked back to our dorm. As usual, I slipped down to the grotto shortly before bed; I don't recall what I would have prayed about—possibly forgiveness for being completely baked—but I seem to remember a deep tranquillity.

And that was our nightly routine for the next few weeks—minus our brush with the priest. We watched the dark patches along our path with paranoid precision, lest some specter of a monk manifest and give us a more thorough grilling than what we'd received from Father X——.

As one might expect, these evening strolls eventually took a toll on my academic performance. It would be quite convenient to place blame on the weed and the beer, but Cody and Ken both maintained A averages. My slipping grades never entered into my covert praying, though. When I knelt to pray before the statue of the Holy Mother, I typically prayed for guidance. Or I prayed for people that I knew or didn't know. I avoided that oldest of prayers, the one about deliverance.

My falling GPA landed me in Father X——'s office. In addition to teaching, he was also the academic student liaison—the guy you saw before you saw the dean.

"So out with it, Mr. Keck. What's causing the old slump?

Too much amateur astronomy?" He began to guffaw in his Santa-like manner. I wasn't immediately sure what he was referring to, and when I figured it out, I was unable to tell if he knew more than he was letting on.

"No," I said. "I just . . . I just feel a little lost. A little stressed."

"I see. Well, do you pray about these things?"

"Oh, yes, I pray."

"Regularly?"

"Yes."

"Well, do you have friends? Do you get to go out much?"

"I have friends. I don't go out much. You know. Money." I wasn't really poor; I just spent all my money on intoxicants and snack food.

"You should come to more of the events on campus. It's not all keggers!" He gave his belly laugh; I smiled weakly. "But seriously. We show movies on Thursday nights, and it's pretty good stuff. Not all of it is Vatican-approved." I saw that little twinkle in his eye. "We're showing a French film this weekend. *Manon of the Spring*. Do you know it?" I said that I didn't. "Well, you should come see it. Father Arthur is a bit of a stereo nut and he's developed the most spectacular stereo sound for these movies." He paused for a few seconds and just looked at me. "You know, I actually have to go grab something from the movie room. Why don't you come along for a preview? It's sure to convince you to come."

I obediently followed Father X—— down the hall and up two flights of stairs. We didn't talk, and he covered the echo of our footsteps by whistling a nameless tune that reverberated through the corridors of the building. The movies were shown in what was essentially an oversize classroom with a large-screen television at the front of the room. The windows were blacked out with heavy drapes, and the room itself was ringed by some thirty-eight stereo speakers of various ages and dimensions.

I sat in the middle of the room and watched as Father X—— found the movie in question and turned on all the equipment.

Father X—— turned off the lights and took a seat next to me as the movie was beginning. *Manon* begins with the title's namesake, Manon—a waifish blonde ingenue—dancing naked around a well. A half-wit watches her from a ledge.

"Fantastic sound," Father X—— said. "You can hear the water running in the bottom of that well. Hear it?"

I tilted my head so that I appeared to be listening intently. I thought I heard a slight static. I nodded my agreement. Father X—— put his arm along the back of my chair and leaned in to say:

"I'm glad you're in here with me. If someone walked in and I was in here alone watching *this*, well, what would people say!" It was like having Santa Claus make a salacious remark to me; my back was suddenly stiff. Father X—— removed his arm from the back of my chair.

And placed it on my knee.

"Yes, nothing wrong with watching this. It's natural."

And it may have been natural. It might have turned out to be just two guys watching a foreign film in the dark in the afternoon, just casually demonstrating affection with some harmless physical contact. Father X—— had never made me especially nervous—unlike Brother J——, who

had a disturbing leering tendency—and everyone I knew
loved him. He seemed immune from the rumors that circulated about some of the other priests, but the moment his
hand landed on my knee I was up and stumbling over
chairs in the dark as I panted for the door. I heard Father
X—— saying something to me, and I mumbled about having a night class that I needed to study for—he would have
known that there was no such class on my schedule. As
soon as I was in the hallway, I sprinted for the steps and
didn't slow down until I was outside and well away from
the building. My heart was racing wildly and I was certain
I was going to pass out. I took the most expedient route
home that wound me past the grotto—I looked at the Virgin over my shoulder, but I didn't stop.

I went directly into Cody's room when I got back to the
dorm; he and Ken were leaned back in their chairs, surveying their cards. Cody glanced up at me and said:

"You look kind of fucked up, man. You okay?"

"Where's Blue Boy?"

Cody gave a sideways glance to Ken, then reached behind the couch and produced the bong. Ken tossed a bag
into my lap, and I packed the bowl and took a few hits
while Cody and Ken continued their game of gin.

"I'm thinking of changing my major to English," I said.

Cody laid his cards down faceup and looked at me.
"Now that's more like it."

Lamentations

With the exception of a few nights when I had far too much to drink, I can't recall doing any genuine praying after my time at the Abbey until my grandfather's death. People close to me had died before, but the scythe had never struck so close to home. I was shaken. I felt the madness creeping in again. My relationship with Lilith was not going well at all. I didn't know what to do, so I went to church.

At first the prayers were the mumbled memories I'd not recited in a long while: the Apostles' Creed, the Lord's Prayer . . . and I spent the quiet moments of personal reflection wondering just what the fuck I was doing seated among people whom I considered to be only a glass of Kool-Aid away from total insanity.

Holy Nada, in Whom I do not believe, throw me a bone here. If you exist, if you are listening, if you aren't too fucking busy ignoring the suffering of the children of Africa, could you send me a good woman? Because I've been trying. I've been giving it my best shot, and I feel like I need a little bonus here, like a hot set of twins or something. Also, if you pay attention to this prayer and not all the ones about stopping the war, you've really got to get your priorities in order . . . And I know you've probably been hearing this a lot lately after the Red Sox sweeping the series, but what about the Cubs?

I stared at the mute cross that floated above the pulpit; it was suspended by thin wires to create that mystical illusion, and I found myself wishing those wires would snap and the cross impale the minister. And not because I had any disdain for the minister—he's genuinely one of the truest Christians I've ever met. It's just that I was in the mood for an Old Testament God, the proactive one with a taste for arson and a gambler's sensibility. The one who knew how to send a message. This New Testament God, with his warm-fuzzies approach, really sucked. "Turn the other cheek," Jesus advised. Where were my locusts, my plague of retribution?

At the end of the service, before I'd even had time to rise from the pew, a woman's voice said:

"Kevin?"

I turned around; an attractive brunette in her late thirties was staring at me. I began to mentally recant all the blasphemous statements I'd ever made in my life. These were incredibly fast results.

"Hi." I didn't know what else to say. I assumed she knew the reason why she was talking to me, and she did:

"Do you think you'd be interested in teaching our high school Sunday school class? We're having a tough time finding someone who will stick with it, and your name was suggested to me."

I looked down in my lap at the church bulletin and began to fold and refold it into a tiny square of waste. My honest thought at the moment was *Well, if I don't do it, they'll probably end up with some right-wing wacko who teaches them to hate fags and abortionists.* I was so baffled by the request to have me lead a Sunday school class that I wasn't struck by the curiosity of the timing until I was firing up a joint on the drive back home.

The following Sunday I woke up two hours before I had to be at the church. I took a bong hit—several, actually—and considered what I was going to tell a group of high school kids about Christianity. If someone stopped me on the street and asked for a lesson in Christian doctrine, I'd say, "It's fairly fucked-up. But try to be nice to everyone. That's about all you need to know." I doubted that would go over well at the church.

I tried to recall my own Sunday school classes from when I was younger, but all I could think of was a craft activity in which one used yarn, glitter, and construction paper to make the animals of Noah's Ark. And even though all of those items could be found in my apartment, there was no way I was leading a craft activity.

The high school kids had their Sunday school class in what was known as the Youth Room. It earned its name because the room had couches and a foosball table. Clearly, comfortable seating and table soccer is the line of demarcation between adolescence and adulthood. Perhaps not so strangely, I felt right at home.

When I arrived at the classroom, I found four people waiting on me. They were sitting on a single sofa. I stared at the faces in front of me. A father and his three children. Obviously, someone had made them come to the class so I'd have someone to talk to. The father, a deacon in our church, was present for reconnaissance purposes. The children appeared to be there because they'd been threatened.

I attempted to use all my stalling tactics that I use on the first day of my literature courses. I asked everyone's name and where they were from. In a college class this works out well because I'm dealing with a diverse group of individuals. With four people who are related it's an icebreaker that sinks quickly.

I picked up a Bible that was lying beside me on the couch.

"Is anyone familiar with Ecclesiastes?"

The quartet shook their heads side to side solemnly.

"Well," I said as I flipped to the proper page, "let's talk about vanity," and I proceeded to monologue for thirty minutes on the pointlessness of life. The basic premise of Ecclesiastes might be summed up this way: you're going to die, there's nothing you can do about it, you will never understand the world and what it means, thus you should just sit back, relax, get a good woman, and love her as hard as you can. *Vanity of vanities! All is vanity!* That was how the book began. It was an idea that was heavy on my mind. Over the preceding few weeks I'd watched the sum of a man's life reduced to a few boxes of photographs and mementos.

When I concluded my talk about Ecclesiastes, the kids were all staring at their shoes. The father slapped his hands on his knees, stood, shook my hand, and said, "Good stuff. Uplifting." He didn't seem the type of person inclined to nuanced sarcasm, so I accepted that he was sincere. His kids followed him out of the room without a word to me. I spent the worship service in the Youth Room practicing foosball on the church's criminally underused table.

The following Sunday I expected—perhaps even prayed—to find an empty room welcoming me. Alas, the same three siblings were there, but they'd brought a few friends. A tiny portion of me wanted to explain to them how uncool it is to invite people to church—but maybe church had become hip and I was unaware. I doubted it, but I wasn't willing to risk the ridicule of a group of teenagers. This time, though, no deacon was overseeing me, and so I settled back into a couch and talked for forty-five minutes about the problems of free will in a universe controlled by physical laws.

When I was done, a sixteen-year-old girl named Wendy said, "So, like, what does this have to do with Jesus?"

I didn't have an immediate answer. As I was a little baked, and therefore a little snackish, I'd started thinking about the possibility of a grilled cheese in my future.

"Well, you know, Wendy . . . Okay. Here it is: Because you're made of the same basic molecules as everything else in the universe, you're subject to the laws of physics, and yet it seems as though we're immune from that because we make choices. Or seem to. So are we making choices, or are our choices really just the result of forces in the universe acting upon us?"

"Well, duh," she said, leaning forward and shaking her head at me. "Of course some force is acting on us. We call that the Holy Spirit."

I looked around the room. The other kids were nodding

in agreement. I picked up a Bible and threw it at Wendy's head. She was quicker than she looked and batted it down before it made contact.

"What are you doing? Are you freaking crazy?"

"No, I just want to ask you a question: did I decide to throw that Bible or did the Holy Spirit make me do it?"

Over the next few weeks more kids would trickle in each Sunday until the couches were filled to capacity. I couldn't figure it out. What we discussed in the Youth Room—evolution, abortion, teen sex, drugs—was so antithetical to typical Christian belief that I expected the Inquisition to visit me at any moment with charges of heresy. This was not the stuff that most parents would be happy about their children hearing at school, let alone church. And my stances on the issues were what you might expect:

Evolution: "You can believe in God and evolution. Darwin did."

Abortion: "It's not a form of birth control, kids. But would you rather use a doctor or a coat hanger?"

Drugs: "All the movies made about marijuana are comedies. Movies about cocaine and heroin are tragedies. If you need it spelled out more definitively than that, I recommend you stay away from drugs."

But the Inquisition never came knocking. In fact, parents stopped me in the corridors and parking lot of the church to tell me what good things they'd heard from their children. I wanted to say, "You realize I'm totally baked? You know I've swallowed more pain pills just this morning than most people would consider advisable in a day?" But my reply was always an embarrassed "Thanks," and then I would walk away as quickly as I could.

I hated for those Sunday mornings to give way to the afternoon. Lilith would be waiting for me at the apartment when I got home, ready to apologize for the night before or pick up the pieces of the argument again. That is, if she was awake. And if she wasn't awake, I would have a few hours of tense solitude, waiting to see what mood she would be wearing when she emerged from the bedroom.

Because of this, those weekly occasions with the kids became such sweet relief. Of course, the satisfaction was only halfhearted. I read in their faces the trust of innocence, and in their parents' faces the optimism of faith; I'd not seen these things in the mirror for a long time. Quite simply, I did not believe as they did, and it seemed rather deceitful to sit among them and feign belief. Yet I couldn't stop; it felt too good.

However, the one thing I never did was bring prayer into the Sunday school class. As I didn't believe in a personal God who was actually listening, I felt leading others in a prayer that appealed to this sensibility would be a cruel mockery. No one said anything about the absence of this universal ritual for several weeks until Polly, a tiny girl who seemed perpetually accident-prone, meekly raised her hand:

"Why don't we ever pray in here?"

I'd been expecting this. "Well, I figure you have enough prayer time at the worship service."

She considered this. Kip, one of the siblings who'd been coming from the beginning, asked, "Do you think you can pray too much?"

"I think there's a point at which it gets repetitive. But it's probably one of the few things you can do to excess without hurting yourself." No one seemed to know what I was talking about, but I chuckled to myself anyway. Polly raised her hand again, and her sleeve dipped down to reveal a purple crescent.

"Why doesn't God answer prayers?"

"I don't have an answer for that. What do you mean?"

"I mean I keep praying and nothing happens. It's like . . ." She stopped. Her lower lip trembled.

I coughed into my fist. "Well."

"It's like no one is listening," she said, and I saw the tears beginning. I wasn't capable of coping. This was only a volunteer position.

"Everyone," I said, "let's help Polly out. Let's pray that Polly's prayer gets answered, and maybe if you have some of your own stuff you want addressed, throw that in there, too." I immediately closed my eyes and dropped my head; I was not open to further discussion.

After what seemed like an appropriate amount of time I raised my head and said, "Okay then. Let's see if that gets results."

All of this mess was circulating in my mind as I was sitting in the sun in that brief interval before my next class. I felt detached from myself—I was teaching literature at a mediocre community college to students who were forced to take the course as part of their graduation requirements. Books are the only constant source of meaning in my life, and my having to lecture about *Walden* to twenty-five completely indifferent students was the very definition of despair. Furthermore, I was teaching Sunday school. That alone was enough to disorient me, and if that wasn't enough, Lilith was always available to slap me silly in one of her drunken fits.

I looked up as one of my literature students was sitting down beside me.

"So, you ever had any absinthe before?"

The comment wasn't completely random; Daryl was a student in my Twentieth-Century American Literature class, and during a lecture on Hemingway I was prompted to explain a reference to absinthe in a short story. He'd been the only other person in the room besides me who knew what it was.

I told him a friend had brought some back from Europe several years before and I'd tried it then.

"Did it fuck you up?" His tone lacked the voyeurism of indulgence one might expect; it had a palpable clinical nature to it.

"I didn't have enough."

"Well, if you ever want some, let me know; I keep it around."

"You like it that much?"

"No, it's . . ." Daryl took a drag from his cigarette and glanced around; we were more or less alone. "I practice vampirism. It's part of a ritual."

I turned my head toward Daryl. He was a stocky country boy with coal black hair and muscles shaped by labor and not the ridiculous repetition of weights; he looked directly into my eyes, and his eyes were the color of slate. I'd gotten used to students telling me completely bizarre and personal things. And even though this was quite possibly in the top three weirdo admissions of all time, I thought it best not to laugh at his confession. But it was hard to ignore that I was sitting directly under the sun with a guy who claimed to be a vampire.

When I didn't say anything, he said, "How old do I look to you?"

"I don't know. Twenty-five?"

"I'm thirty-eight."

"You're older than me."

"Get yourself a woman who treats you right. You'll feel the difference in your blood." He smiled, exposing a mouthful of beautiful white teeth, but he wasn't smiling at me: an elderly woman shuffling along with her arms full of library books had come up beside us.

"Daryl," she said, "we missed you in church last week."

Daryl stood up. "I missed y'all, too, Miss Emmie. I was out of town. Let me take those books for you." He took the books from her and they began to walk in the direction of the library.

I overheard her say, "The grass needs mowing at the house. Think you might could get by this week? Arnold's just getting too old, and with this Indian summer . . ."

Before they were out of earshot Daryl turned back to me. "Think about what I said. If you want to meet a nice girl, I know the place."

I wasn't sure what a churchgoing, grass-mowing vampire might have in mind when he said "nice girl," but as tempting as the offer was, I was fairly sure I didn't want to find out.

When I got home that night, I made the puzzling discovery that my apartment was littered with confetti. Upon closer examination I realized the confetti was actually pages of my journals, which Lilith had taken great care to manufacture into fantastically small pieces. I found a note in the bathroom that read, *Fuck you, faggot.* I also found my toothbrush in the toilet.

Lilith wanted to get married; I didn't; and this was the root of all our problems. I loved her—or thought that I did. In retrospect I realize her beauty charmed me because I did not think of myself as beautiful. The one time we tried to have a civil discussion about our future together, she ended up chasing me around the apartment with a BB gun. After that I dealt with issues via my journal, and Lilith had clearly not liked what she had read, which is essentially what I have just said: I wanted out. I could feel my heart beating in my throat, and I felt a wave of complete anguish. I could get another television, I could replace picture frames, but I could not undo this. I went into my room and pounded my fist on my bed. I was trying to be what I thought a good guy should be—patient, kind, all that fucked-up Corinthians crap—but I really felt like nothing more than a total pansy.

Lilith stayed at her parents' that night, and the next day after class I asked Daryl just what he meant by a "nice girl."

"Come and see for yourself. I'm going there tonight."

"Where?"

"Purgatory."

I considered this. "On a Tuesday?"

I met Daryl at Jackalope's—a bar down the street from my apartment that catered to those who enjoyed trying to watch twenty-seven athletic events at once. It was not my kind of bar, but they had my kind of waitresses, and so I often went there and pined through pints, flirting anemically with each waitress, lusting after their pierced navels and tongues, their hips that sang along with the jukebox. I've found waitresses to be a particularly difficult dating demographic for me, much like strippers: part of their job is to give you a sense of possibility, and it takes a real pro to read the proper signs. I am by no means a pro.

When Daryl arrived, he didn't even order a beer. I couldn't blame him; he was terribly out of place in Jackalope's: he looked as though he were on his way to an upscale meeting of Dungeons & Dragons enthusiasts—leather pants and a leather jacket on top of what could only be described as a pirate shirt. He looked out the window facing the street as he waited for me to finish my drink, and when we stood to leave, he looked at me and said, "I like your shoes."

"Look," I said, once we were in the car. "Where are we going exactly?"

"Purgatory. It's a monthly gathering of the leather and S-and-M community. And other people."

"People like vampires?"

"Yep."

"Don't take this the wrong way, but the vampirism . . . this is a metaphor, right? Like all those girls at Phish shows who dress up like fairies and go around spreading pixie . . ." I trailed off. I'd been watching Daryl as I spoke, and his bright incisors had disappeared behind a grimace.

"It's not a metaphor." He paused while Judas Priest serenaded the gap in conversation. After a few moments he smiled again. "Look, I know you. You're cool. Do yourself a favor and leave that fairy shit out of your conversations where we're going."

"Fair enough." I leaned back in my seat. "So what's with the absinthe?"

"Oh, that. Well, you know it's potent shit. Most people it just fucks up. But it won't even intoxicate a vampire. It's a test, you know. To see if you've got the gene."

"What gene?"

"The vampire gene."

A scientific debate with someone claiming the existence of a vampire gene seemed rather pointless. I let the matter slide.

"So, do you like, you know, bite necks?"

Daryl slowed for a yellow light, and when the car was stopped, he turned to me and said, "Do I look like I have fucking fangs to you?" He flashed his teeth.

"Uh, no."

"Yeah." His face dropped. "It sucks. I just can't afford to have the work done. You'll meet people tonight who've got them. Some are quality dental work. Some just look like crap because people file their teeth—that's just insane. Some people just get lucky by birth . . . But if I could afford them, I'd have them. In the meantime, this works." He reached in his jacket and tossed a small item wrapped in wax paper in my lap; I picked it up. It was a disposable scalpel.

"Oh. So you cut and drink?" I offered a weak chuckle
that came out more as a choke.

"Yep."

My stomach began to churn. I handed the scalpel back
to him as we were pulling into the parking lot of the club
where Purgatory was happening. When we were out of the
car, he put his arm around my shoulder and said, "Tonight
you'll feel like a new man." The leather of his jacket
creaked in my ear. "I really love your shoes," he said again
as we approached the door. "I've been looking for a pair
just like that."

In my daily existence, I am most often dressed like a
nine-year-old on his way to baseball practice: Converse
sneakers, jeans, and a jersey-style T-shirt with three-
quarter-length sleeves. On more formal occasions I might
switch out the jeans for khakis. On chilly nights, or on
what I perceive to be ultraformal occasions, I'll add a dress
shirt (typically a blue oxford) to my ensemble, but as I
never button the shirt, it functions more as a dinner jacket.
As I perceived Purgatory to be an ultraformal event, I was
dressed appropriately—I'd even gone so far as to add black
socks and a matching belt, and it was that leather belt that
was most similar to the wardrobes of the other attendees.
I was surrounded by extras from *Interview with the
Vampire*—or a Renaissance festival. Either way, I felt very
much like the Southern preppy in Count Dracula's court.
As I surveyed the room I thought, *One or more of these
people are very likely carrying a set of twelve-sided dice.*

My mood might tepidly have approached something
close to genuine fear had we been in a place more "dungeon-
esque." However, we were at a bar known for its regular

booking of tribute bands, such as Appetite for Destruction
(Guns N' Roses), Zoso (Led Zeppelin), Nothin' But a
Good Time (Poison), and SkaCago (a curiously popular
Chicago cover band who played everything in a ska style).
A person clad in leather with honest-to-God fangs doesn't
look at all threatening standing in front of a sign advertis-
ing two-for-one Jell-O shooters and $1.50 margaritas on
Fridays.

After we'd paid our ten-dollar cover (it seemed only fitting one should pay a nominal fee to gain entrance to Purgatory), I followed Daryl to the bar and ordered the best
beer available—a Corona for Christ's sake! Oh, Purgatory
indeed! I discreetly popped two Percocets in my mouth,
crunched them up, and washed them down with that most
mediocre of Mexican concoctions. I would rather have
gone outside and smoked a bowl, but Daryl didn't exude
the pleasant indifference of a weed aficionado. Besides, at
the bar, he'd ordered a Red Bull. The one time I ordered a
Red Bull I was up until five a.m. crapping a substance that I
thought was certainly a harbinger of hospitalization. That
alone was proof enough for me that people who drink that
stuff are wired differently than I am.

Daryl stood at such a distance from me that it was un-
certain whether we actually knew each other. I've no doubt
that my khakis were the source of his discomfort. I sat on
a barstool and waited for the warm bliss of the Percs to
wash over me and watched as the medievally clad crowd
circulated and exchanged greetings. Nine Inch Nails
played over the PA at a conversation-friendly volume, and
two people who seemed more on the druid side of things
arranged a chair and a coffee table onstage.

When people saw Daryl, they gave a slight bow or curtsy, according to their gender. In every case his reply was a terse nod. Whenever their eyes fell on me, they all appeared to snarl. I smiled politely and raised my Corona.

This went on for some time, and as no one was speaking to me—including Daryl—I was soon tipping back my third Corona and considering a cab ride home. Nine Inch Nails had given way to something resembling the sounds of a genocidal massacre mixed with asphalt production, and it was decidedly not conversation-friendly. The scene seemed a terrible waste of a buzz, and I felt as though I were literally buzzing. Humming, in fact.

A petite girl with purple streaks in her hair and ample piercings walked over to Daryl and curtsied. He smiled at her and opened his arms; when he embraced her, he pressed his face into her neck. In addition to her thin black dress and dog collar, she was wearing a pair of bright white Keds that glowed under the black lights.

Daryl yelled at the girl, "This is my friend, Kevin." The veins in his neck stood out, but he was still barely audible over the music. I leaned my head close to theirs.

"Heaven?" she said.

"Kevin," Daryl repeated.

"Oh." She turned to me and smiled and curtsied again.

Daryl pressed his lips to my ear. "Okay, you're all set. I've got stage business. I'll see you later. Or maybe not." He gave me what I can only characterize as a wicked smile. I grabbed his arm before he could walk away.

"What? What? Where are you going?"

"I'm going to the stage. Amanda is yours for the night. I set it all up. She'll treat you right."

"How do you know her?"

He smiled at me again. "She's a good source of food." I let go of his arm and he pressed into the crowd.

As soon as he was gone, Amanda leaned into me. "I like your shoes."

"Oh, yeah. Thanks. I like yours, too. They glow."

She looked down in wide-eyed amazement. "Oh, they do, don't they?"

"Can I buy you a drink?"

"I don't drink." She had the most wonderful dimples when she smiled, a shy way of looking down. I almost missed it because of the piercings.

"You don't drink? My God, how do you stand it?"

That bashful smile again. "I try to keep my body clean for others."

"Really? You looked like a dirty girl to me." It was my turn to smile. Oh, yes: I was flowing with the buzz, reaching into my bag of tricks. In the glow of neon beer signs it was hard to tell if she was blushing.

She looked me dead in the eye. "When you fuck me, choke me."

This was far outside the scope of my bag of tricks. I smiled at her and flagged the bartender to bring me another Corona. Then the lights went dim and Amanda said, "Oh, it's time for Daryl."

We both turned to the stage. The music was lowered and a voice emanated from the darkness:

"Creatures of darkness"—honestly, this was how it began—"welcome to Purgatory!" The crowd cheered and howled. "Tonight, for your pleasure, our own Lord Moltor presents a live demonstration in which he brings a virgin

over to"—there was a significant pause here—"the darkness!" The crowd howled again, and Daryl appeared onstage escorting a raven-haired woman in a white dress. I
started to say something to Amanda, but the voice erupted
from the PA system again. "I forgot to mention that Lord
Moltor is a licensed phlebotomist. Please do not attempt to
replicate his demonstration at home unless you are under
the supervision of a health-care professional. Thank you."
Daryl—Lord Moltor—helped the woman lie back on the
coffee table, and he took a seat on the throne behind her.
As he did so, the music began again, a slow, pulsing rhythm
that was deliberately aimed at heightening the dramatic
tension of whatever dinner-theater production they were
putting on. Daryl raised the woman's arm so that her wrist
faced the audience. Then he produced a scalpel, and most
of the crowd applauded and whistled.

I didn't want to find out if I was about to see the real
deal or not. Simulated bloodletting is only slightly more
appealing than the actual act, and neither ranks very high
for me. Blood doesn't bother me, knives do not bother me,
but when a knife is finely splitting flesh to draw out blood,
I simply can't handle it. Needles impact me the same way;
whenever I watch a movie and it contains a scene of someone being injected, I have to avert my eyes. I've no doubt I
will die of arterial disease because a cholesterol test is far
too frightening for me to face.

I leaned down to Amanda's ear; metal brushed my lips.
"I need to go outside." I didn't wait for her response.

I staggered through the crowd toward the exit. It
was cool outside, and I took deep gulps of air. I could feel
the spit welling up in my mouth, and I stumbled into the

parking lot and pressed my hands against the hood of a car to steady myself. I lay my face against the cool metal, but I heaved and threw up anyway.

"Are you okay?" It was Amanda. Her hand was on my back. I slumped against the side of the car embarrassed and incredibly inebriated. "If you want, we can just go back to my place and you can rest. Maybe you had too much to drink." She had the most benevolent smile.

"That sounds nice." I wiped my mouth on the back of my sleeve. She held out her hand to help me up, and that's when I saw the raised scar on her forearm, and then I saw what it spelled: *Daryl*. I leaned over and puked again. And then several times more. When I looked up, Amanda was gone.

I sifted through my vomit for portions of pills, found half of an undigested Percocet, and popped it in my mouth. I had enough postnausea salivation going on that it was easy to swallow. I reached in my pocket for my cell to call a cab, and I began to laugh. There was no reason to fear bloodthirsty vampires at all: I'd forgotten I had my rosary.

When the cab dropped me off, I went in through the front door of my apartment. Normally I always used the back door, which connects the kitchen to the fire escape, but it was a blind turn from the kitchen into the living room, and I'd been surprised before by one of Lilith's stealthy attacks. I wanted a little space to prepare a defense if things ended up going down that way. It seemed likely that they would. I'd been gone long enough that Lilith had sufficient time to work herself into a good lather over something trivial.

I slid my key into the lock as quietly as possible and

opened the door. It seemed to creak louder than usual, and I stepped quickly into the apartment and closed it behind me. I'd expected the crepuscular glow of the television, but everything was dark. I took a few steps and stopped. The refrigerator hummed contently in the kitchen. A cat's claws picked at the fabric of the couch, and when the cat jumped down and started toward me, I heard it again. I waited for Lilith's voice or the floor to squeak under her footsteps. When my eyes finally adjusted to the pale illumination of the room from the streetlamp outside the window, it made sense: things were missing, and what I was hearing was the echo of open space.

The cat began to purr in time with the refrigerator. I didn't bother to look for a note, but instead sat down and stretched out on the bare floor and thought about Lilith. In the empty room awash with pale light, answers were beginning to take shape.

Chronicles

A few months after I'd broken up with Lilith, she sent this text message to my cell phone: *I just want u 2 no I slept w/ Julius while u &I were still dating. That's right, we had sex. Revenge is a dish best served cold.*

She actually said that thing about revenge—I wish that were some terrible cliché that bubbled up from my poor imagination, but instead it's a terrible cliché from a woman with whom I had sex for three years. For quite a while I was unsure whether it was the content of her message or the phrasing that upset me most.

Julius was not only a friend who lived across the street and a trusted companion, but also a preacher's son. That last item should immediately have raised a red flag that he was going to cause trouble. As all Protestants know, the children of clergy are as savagely mischievous as their parent-of-the-cloth is pious. Catholics don't really have this problem, but in their prohibition against procreation for their priests they've whipped up an entirely different issue.

Truthfully, though, I couldn't have cared any less that Julius had nailed Lilith. She and I were through, so any sense of betrayal on my part was moot. Besides, she and

Julius and I had spent the night in question drinking and joking around about the possibility of a three-way, but because of the bong I became narcoleptic rather early. What ultimately got to me was the realization that, once again, my dream of group sex had come so close to fulfillment, but instead of orgiastic ecstasy I am left only with the memory of a sweet, solitary slumber. Story of my life. Also, the night was a bitter reminder that Lilith had dangled the prospect of group sex before in the past, and it had also been an exercise in humiliation.

We'd been invited to the house of Lilith's dental hygienist for New Year's Eve. "They're swingers," Lilith told me when I initially resisted going; I wasn't a big fan of parties with Lilith's friends. She knew I felt I was missing something essential about life in regards to my ever-elusive group fantasy. She'd previously told me that she would do anything I wanted if I presented her with an engagement ring. I nearly asked her why she'd dropped this relationship clause, but instead I played it as cool as I possibly could, given that fulfillment of a lifelong dream was so close. Also, I was happy to have the ring subject dropped *period*. In the preceding months, Lilith had relentlessly been dropping hints that what she wanted more than anything else in this world for Christmas was an engagement ring. A lot of this pressure emanated from her mother, a Charlotte socialite who adhered to the quaint notion that a girl was destined to be an old maid if she wasn't wed by the age of twenty-five. Lilith was teetering on the brink of spinsterhood, and thus if we were watching television and a commercial for a jeweler's came on, she'd comment along the lines of "That's a pretty ring—that's the sort of ring *I'd like.*" Even if she was in another room when the advertisements commenced, she would step into the doorway for the duration *just in case* a commercial featuring engagement rings came on. Perhaps she thought she was being subtle, but it's difficult to fail to notice that someone only provides commentary when a specific piece of jewelry flashes on the screen; it was a Pavlovian response to be marveled at, which I would have had I not been the target of her programming.

Besides, even if I had the desire to be married, I certainly didn't have the money; I taught college part-time, and that's enough to eek out an existence for me. I don't see why I should work hard to own a home and drive a nice car, or the point of winning any sort of game, when we're all just going to end up dead anyway. Why bother? Better to spend your time like Thoreau, working as little as possible and doing as much of what you like while you're here. Such an attitude prevents one from accumulating the capital necessary to purchase precious metals, but it does offer the luxury of acquiring a gift card to Target, and as Lilith liked buying knickknacks for the apartment, I thought that a gift with the possibility for fulfilling a variety of desires was a splendid idea.

Lilith and I started out the door around nine on New Year's Eve to walk to the party; winter is often nonexistent in North Carolina, and so the evening was only mildly chilly. As we turned the corner, I put my hand on Lilith's ass; she was wearing a black cocktail dress that made her look especially fuckable. A voice from a passing car yelled,

"Woohoo!" and then that car stopped just ahead of us. I recognized it: it was my brother's.

He rolled down the passenger's window and said, "What up, dude? I thought I'd missed you."

I leaned down and put my head in the car. "We just got started. Some friends of Lilith's are having a party."

"Cool, I was hoping you had something planned."

I turned my head to look at Lilith; she'd lit a cigarette and was giving me the wide-eyed stare of *No, absolutely no way is he coming.* I put my head back in the car. "I don't know, dude. You may not be dressed properly." My brother was sporting shorts, a tie-dyed T-shirt, sandals, and a thick hemp necklace. He'd been cultivating a beard for months, though perhaps *cultivation* is a misleading term; he was growing a wild, hairy beast on his face.

"What the fuck, man? It's tradition that we spend New Year's together."

This was not exactly true. My brother and I had spent the previous New Year's Eve together, but that was it. His habit was to declare anything that had occurred once a tradition if he wanted to do it again. This was not some weird revisionist history that he deployed as a way to imbue one with guilt and get his way; he was not as clever as our mother in that regard. He was sincere, and for this reason I looked back at Lilith and made an apologetic face while simultaneously fighting the urge to grab my brother's keys from the ignition and hurl them into the bushes and take off running with Lilith. But she had heels on, and Brandon was, after all, my younger brother. I opened the car door for her and he drove us the few blocks to Karen and Harry's.

Karen and Harry lived in a modest cottage in the Plaza

Midwood neighborhood, just across the railroad tracks and down past the Penguin restaurant. We appeared to be the early arrivals, as the house did not give off the appearance of being in full swing. Harry, a fellow about the same age as me, with dark hair and a chiseled, gymnast look, answered the door. He was wearing roughly the same clothing as my brother.

"Lilith!" he exclaimed as he opened the door. He pulled her into a tight embrace and kissed her full on the lips. I thought this was a bit inappropriate, swinger or not, then he suddenly released Lilith and swept me into a deep bear hug, kissing both of my cheeks and saying, "And you must be Kevin! It's so good to meet you—Karen and I have heard so much about you." When he let me go, he was beaming with a warm, friendly smile, but there was something *too friendly* about it that made me uneasy. His smile quickly collapsed into puzzlement when I stepped aside and my brother, who had been loitering in the background on the front porch, moved to make his way in the house.

"And you are . . . ?" Harry trailed off.

"Oh, I'm sorry. This is my brother, Brandon." I offered no further explanation, and Harry stuck his head out the door and glanced both ways.

"Just the three of you?"

"Yep." I looked around for Lilith; she had disappeared.

"Ah, okay. Well . . ." Harry stuck out his hand to my brother. "Nice to have you, Brandon. Come in and have a beer."

My brother said, "Cool," but I had distinctly detected in Harry's tone that it was not cool at all. Not by a long shot.

Harry and Karen's home seemed like one catalog photo after another: every item in every room was carefully chosen and placed. It did not feel like an actual home, but rather a model of what the home of a twenty-first-century, young, urban, professional couple should look like. When Harry opened the refrigerator, I noticed everything inside it seemed arranged: things lined up in an unnatural way. The beers were in rows; the cottage cheese, sour cream, and cream cheese were placed in order of descending size. A menagerie of anonymous Tupperware containers was also separated by size. The condiments in the refrigerator door: sized. At one time in my life such tidiness would have made me feel as though I had encountered my soul mates, but there was something fucked-up about neat-freak swingers.

I mentioned to Harry how nice his house was, but he dismissed the comment as though he'd heard it all before, saying only, "Yeah, it's okay. Karen decorates. You guys want a bong hit?" He opened the freezer and took out three quart-size mason jars, then reached into the cupboard and removed an ornate bong standing about eighteen inches high. My uneasiness began to subside significantly.

"So what we got here," Harry said as he opened the jars, "is AK-47, Trinity, and Northern Lights. What do you want to start with?"

Start with? Harry had just announced he had three varieties of high-grade weed—weed that had a *name*. When marijuana has a name, prepare for the complete annihilation of reason. I consider myself a cultured smoker of pot, but I don't have the connections to rendezvous with the contraband Harry presented as though it were merely a series of frozen dinners. I was worried that I might not even remember the impending orgy.

Harry packed a sample of each variety for me and my brother, and as we worked our way through each numbing hit, I heard the laughter of women emanating from a doorway. Occasionally their tittering was punctuated by a deeper voice, and I said to Harry, "Who else is here?"

"Greg and Brittany. Lilith is probably downstairs with them and Karen."

"Oh, so we're not the first to arrive."

"Nope, you're last. I guess that makes you *it*." Harry winked at me, then put the bong to his mouth as he filled it with smoke and inhaled. My brother smiled at me.

"Last? Isn't anyone else coming?"

Harry exhaled as he spoke, making his voice sound strained. "No, it's just the six of us—well"—he tilted his head toward my brother as he looked at me—"seven. We like to keep these things, you know, intimate." He winked at me again, then began packing up the bong for another round; my legs and arms tingled. I felt that I needed to speak or I would forget how to talk, so I did my best to make cocktail chatter:

"So Lilith tells me that Karen's a hygienist; what do you do?"

"I work at the bank. B of A."

"Cool. What do you do there?"

"I market credit cards and high-interest loans to families and individuals who have a history of managing their debt while accumulating more revolving accounts. It's a lucrative market for banking right now, because so many workers—particularly low-wage earners—are conscientious, you know? We market to *pride*. That's a really fresh market. What do you do?"

"I teach."

"Tough market. Teachers are a high credit risk—tough for them to work more than one job to cover the bills, you know?" He turned to my brother. "You?"

"I live at home."

"Loyalty. Good market. Parents are good about picking up the tab. You have a credit card?"

"I use my dad's." My brother's unflinching honesty about his dependent situation at the age of twenty-four embarrassed me, most likely because it had only too recently been that I was equally dependent on our parents' good graces, and I was much older.

Harry handed the bong to me as he addressed my brother. "Think about getting your own. If your dad banks with us, we can tie your card into his account, and you'll never have to worry about the bills with the bank—you two can work out some arrangement." After passing my brother the bong, Harry said, "Well, let's go downstairs. That's where the real party is." And then as an afterthought to my brother: "Remind me to give you my card before you leave to give to your dad; I'll get you both a better interest rate." My brother nodded with sincerity.

The downstairs of Karen and Harry's house looked precisely as the basement of a swinger's house should: it had a large leather sofa, a recliner, a large-screen television, a bar, and a beanbag chair. The lighting was dim, and a glass-top coffee table operated as a buffet for lines of co- caine.

Lilith was downstairs, as Harry had suggested; she was sitting next to a brunette who was wearing jeans and a tank top. Another couple—a guy who looked similar to Harry (chiseled, athletic) and a thin, doll-like blonde— were standing at the bar. Everyone stopped talking when we got to the bottom of the steps.

"Well, the gang's all here," said Harry, and walked off to the bar to make a drink.

My brother and I stood in the room, everyone staring at us. My perception of time was warped, so it seemed as if several minutes passed before I raised my hand and said, "Hi, I'm Kevin." I jerked my thumb at my brother. "This is my brother." I looked at my brother; he grinned at the room. "Brandon. That's his name."

The brunette stuck her hand out toward me; I had to take a few steps forward to reach it. "Hi, Kevin, I'm Karen." When she smiled, it was sheer radiance. It was easy to see why she'd been a model; she exuded a classic beauty, somewhat like Audrey Hepburn.

The other couple introduced themselves as Greg and Brittany. Greg was in advertising; Brittany was a catalog model. (Yes, indeed, sweet God in heaven, *two* models!) They both had perfect teeth, but when Brittany spoke, it sounded as though she had just inhaled a balloonful of cig- arette smoke and helium.

After the introductions, everyone went back to what he or she was doing: conversing and pretending as though my brother and I weren't there. Harry was surveying the drink

he had just made, and Brandon and I clung close to him at
the bar. He said, "You two want a beer?" We did, and as
he handed me mine, he said in a low voice, "You know, I
think we have a lot in common."

"Yeah?" I said.

"Yeah, Lilith's told me and Karen about you. But, you
know, when we start getting naked, your brother has to
hang upstairs. Nothing personal."

"It's cool. He'll be all right."

"Cool. Let's do some blow." And with that he slapped
me on my back and made his way across the room to the
coffee table.

Perhaps I am a bit of a prude where cocaine is concerned, but I have little tolerance for its use. This could be
viewed as hypocritical from a person who believes, as the
late Bill Hicks did, that smoking marijuana should not
only be legal but mandatory. So, the party happening
downstairs was minus two participants: me and my
brother; Lilith liked her coke on holidays (another point of
contention between us), and I'd quietly explained to Harry
that I was taking Brandon upstairs to give him the low-
down for the night, but it gave me a worthy excuse to escape a scene with which I was uncomfortable. True, all the
hot women were down there, snorting lines, and it seemed
as though the blow was an aphrodisiac to the group festivities, but Brandon and I had three quart-size mason jars
full of name-brand weed in front of us. After a few tokes
any disappointments with the direction the night was taking were easily forgotten, and besides, I would join them
when they were ready.

My brother and I remained upstairs for quite a while,

occasionally punctuating the silence between us with half-baked musings on the dilemma of free will in a universe subject to physical laws, or the dilemma of "Freebird" versus "Stairway to Heaven." My brother's background in philosophy and physics isn't as strong as mine, but he's as well versed as I am in music, and when I spotted an acoustic guitar in the corner, I immediately took it up and began to play the opening few verses of each song so that a detailed analysis might be made. As I was pointing out to Brandon that each tune could be said to adhere to Poe's "Philosophy of Composition," Karen emerged at the top of the steps. She had changed into a long, flowing nightgown with a neckline that plunged in a thin V-shape to her navel; the bottom half of the gown was slit on both sides up to her thighs.

Marijuana—particularly the kind that has a pedigree—doesn't exactly make one a quick wit. While it is easy to slip into lengthy and painfully detailed digressions about music, the cosmos, or cookie dough, sudden changes in one's setting tend to be addressed with a degree of slowness and stupidity. Sadly, it was my brother who spoke first and said, "Damn."

I quickly snapped to attention (more than just mentally), lest Brandon's obviousness derail the night in some unforeseen fashion. "Are we having a slumber party?"

"I heard you playing the guitar." Karen crossed the room, her nightgown trailing after her as thin veil of mist, and sat beside me. Her bare thigh brushed against me. "I really like the way you play."

"Thanks." I could achieve no greater response than

that, as the blood had suddenly drained from my brain and was in rapid transit to lower circulatory regions.

"Why don't you come down and play with us now." She purred those words in such a tantalizing way that she could have been inviting me to my death and I would have gone along just as willingly. But it was not my death I was going to: I was being ushered into a basement where I would have sex with two models (well, one was a former model, but still . . .) and it was totally okay. I could not be punished for it, and better yet I didn't have to buy an engagement ring. I was also stoned senseless on the most premium weed I'd ever smoked. Life was grand. I followed Karen to the top of the steps, where she turned and looked at my brother and said, "Why don't you come, too? We've never had brothers here."

I was a little taken aback by this, but more so by my brother's reaction: given the chance to have sex with a model in the same room as me, I was sure he'd bail out just as I would. *Thanks but no thanks.* Instead he practically leaped over the plush sofa and began to follow us downstairs, grinning wildly and not saying a word.

In the basement everyone was seated in a rough approximation of a circle, chattering loudly and laughing. A large sheet of plastic lay on the floor. The cocaine and the coffee table were gone, and as we entered the room, Harry said, "Hey, I thought—," but Karen cut him short, saying, "We've never had brothers." Harry just shrugged his shoulders and seemed to quickly forget about it, saying only:

"Well, Greg, let's show them how it's done." Harry stood and took off his shirt and looked at my brother and me. "Gentlemen first, boys. That's how we do it for the ladies here." If it got the girls hot, I didn't mind stripping down for their pleasure; my brother was hesitant and sat immobile while I stood and disrobed. I admit it was awkward having him there, and it didn't help my penis presentation one bit. His presence kept my dick limp and tiny, and when I looked at him, he just shook his head and chuckled. Harry and Greg were greasing themselves with baby oil. With the exception of their heads, their bodies were hairless, and they had the toned look of men who spend unreasonable amounts of time at a gym. Harry said, "Come on, Brandon, no stragglers. Kevin, grease it up. You'll be next."

I picked up the baby oil and stared at it, perplexed, then looked at the rug of hair on my chest—it was going to be an ugly mess momentarily. And then I said, "Next for what?"

"This!" Greg shouted, and flung his naked body into Harry's, whereupon they collapsed into a pile on the plastic, their cocks stiffening as they each tried to wrestle the other into submission. My brother stood up and left the basement quickly.

The women watched attentively, completely disinterested in my thin, greaseless frame, but enthralled by the scene taking place before them: two hunky men slipping over each other, occasionally grabbing the other's cock and yanking on it as they maneuvered through some bizarre homoerotic, hand-job wrestling match. To say that I was mortified would be an extreme understatement.

I looked at Lilith, who smiled demurely at me, then I gazed at the tangle of Harry and Greg on the floor. Without looking at me Harry reached up and put his hand on my thigh; I felt my penis trying to shrink into my ab-domen. Harry's hand was stroking Greg's cock as they wrestled, and they paused in their struggle simultaneously as Harry addressed me, his hand never ceasing its up-and-down motion:

"Hey, man, what's wrong? You think this is some sort of gay thing? The girls just like a good show, man. It's not a gay thing—our wives are right here watching. We just like to wrestle and fondle each other because it gets them hot. There's nothing gay about this, and when they get hot, we fuck them and we watch each other—it's all good."

I was confused, but not by his reasoning: I believed what he said about this whole scene not being gay; sexual-ity is far too complicated to be defined by whether you love to stroke someone else's cock, and however poorly phrased his argument may have been, he was essentially right.

Be that as it may, none of this changed my own stance on cock stroking: I like mine, and I don't like it being stroked by anyone else who has one. The thought neither repulses nor arouses me; it is the same indifference I have when I think of the Style section of the newspaper: who cares?

I was willing to sit through this portion of the festivities, feigning interest (but not participating), as long as I was fucking the hot wives shortly thereafter. I clarified this point to make sure there wasn't a requirement of involve-ment in the first act of the floor show:

"You mean you fuck each other's wives while you watch, but you don't have to—"

I didn't have a chance to finish my question before Harry stopped jerking on Greg's cock and looked at me grimly. "No, man. That's kind of fucked-up. I've got more respect for my wife than to let some other dude fuck her." He looked at Greg. "No offense."

"None taken. I feel you."

In the midst of this discussion I'd missed Lilith's exit from the room; the wives were holding hands on the couch and sipping their drinks, bright-eyed with their husbands' declaration of spousal devotion. These were some coke-snorting, Greek-wrestling nutcases, and they had also drawn a line in the sand: it just happened to be a little further out than mine. I stood slowly and said, "Would you all excuse me for a moment?" I headed back up the stairs, scooping my clothing from the floor as I did so. Before I reached the top of the staircase I heard Harry's merciless pumping of Greg's member begin again as Harry said, "What a fucking dick." I wasn't confused at all by his meaning.

My brother was staring at the television not at all like a person who is actually watching TV, but rather like a person who is looking at the television to avoid seeing his brother naked.

As I dressed, I said, "Where's Lilith?"

"Outside smoking." His answer was robotic.

"Get your shit together; we're about to leave."

"Man, I've *had* my shit together."

Outside, Lilith was smoking with hurried puffs, trying to repress a small, smug smile. She and I stood in the aura of the porch light while my brother walked to the car.

"What the fuck was that, Lilith?" I was more genuinely puzzled than pissed; marijuana has a way of doing that.

She inhaled deeply, then exhaled as she turned to me

and said coolly, "I said to buy me a ring, fucker, and I'd do anything you wanted, and what did you do? You gave me a fifty-dollar gift card to Target." She puffed her cigarette again. "Besides, I thought you'd like that shit."

I stared toward the sky, but the streetlights obscured the tapestry of stars that I knew to be shimmering overhead. "Target has some nice stuff," I said, and walked to the car, Lilith not far behind me.

Eventually Lilith's urgent desire to be married would manifest in an unceasing passive-aggressive rage, the culmination of which was her revelation about sleeping with my neighbor Julius. But it would be nearly a year before that would happen. In the meantime, I accepted her anger because she was hot and knew how to make me come. It all seemed completely worthwhile when I was in the thick of it.

But on that morning, my brother and I left Lilith at my apartment and took off in his car on the pretense of getting some breakfast. We drove downtown and through the city; the barricades marking the party from hours before had been set aside, the streets mostly swept clean—small bits of trash and confetti still clung to the sidewalks as a light dusting of snow. Aside from the few people who were still obligated to be at work, the roads were empty except for the two of us. We drove past the bank buildings that towered toward heaven, the gleaming new apartments like mushrooms sprouting up around them, the churches that hunkered humbly in the city's steel canyons, and we kept driving until the wide boulevards of asphalt dwindled to a trickle of road that wound us to a fist of rock rising from the earth.

We left our car outside the gate to the park and took the

shorter trail to the summit of Crowders Mountain; the sky was violet, and a thin ribbon of white buffered the edge of the horizon, broken only by my city standing erect and mute in the distance. I saw the half-moon still lingering, and I looked for the brightest star in the sky but was met with a band of shimmering satellites. I thought of the astronauts circling the earth at that precise moment in the International Space Station. Does the mania of fireworks sparkle beyond the stratosphere? And whom do the astronauts kiss at midnight, and who cares anyway? I suspect that hovering above the earth, one ceases to be concerned about earthly things; the body begins to lose muscle mass when it's in space: detached from the soil that holds us firm, we begin to disintegrate, to fade into the universe. I imagine the mind losing its sense of itself, the disparity of fantasy and reality finally merging, until dreams sweep up the missing molecules of the body and the cosmos ripples as the surface of a still lake broken by the return of a stone.

Acts

Of course, Lilith didn't disappear from my life as simply as her possessions vanished from my apartment. We'd broken up and gotten back together so many times that this occasion seemed yet another spin in the cycle. We saw each other infrequently through the holidays and into the New Year, but something was definitely different in her attitude, as though she was consciously trying to teach me a lesson and break me once and for all.

I feel I have perhaps painted Lilith as evil incarnate. You know, insightful reader, that I've been quite selective of the events concerning Lilith that are herein recorded. I've not told you, for instance, that I came home one day after work that first December living on Clement Avenue, and Lilith had set up a Christmas tree in my apartment and adorned it with decorations she'd made herself. Who had ever done anything for me that so genuinely expressed a Christmas spirit, that wasn't forced, that neither demanded nor required anything in return? If that wasn't love, I don't know what is.

Still, I changed the locks when she left after my interlude with the vampire. I felt she was plotting. Her typical tactic was to go out and sleep with someone else, but usually this was a retaliation for my own brand of infidelities—Lilith was determined that I would not spend my seed on Internet porn and deny her pleasures; when she felt this was getting out of hand, she had no problem demonstrating what lengths she would go to so as to ensure she was getting laid to her satisfaction.

The problem was that I really and truly didn't care if she did that. (In fact, I kind of liked her telling me about it when we had sex.) It wasn't because I didn't love Lilith, but love seemed like something unquantifiably deeper than just the ability to be monogamous. Had she been out banging a different dude every night, that would have been another matter, but to transgress a few times a year seemed a stupid thing to hold against someone. All I'd heard about my whole life, especially in church, when it came to relationships was this notion of *unconditional love*, but everywhere I looked, people were laying down the conditions.

I know that unconditional love is possible because I'd watched my grandfather care for my grandmother until the business of dying overtook him completely—I personally witnessed his suffering, of which he thought nothing, simply because he loved his wife.

And also I own cats. This is a rather trivial thing compared to my grandfather's actions, but bear with me on this one. Whereas other animals (here I speak specifically of dogs) tend to give unconditional love no matter the owner's disposition, cats expect unconditional love from their owners. (And I hesitate to even suggest a cat can be owned, because I've had at least one cat decide he liked someone else's lodgings better and merely trotted out the door one day with his favorite toy in his mouth, never to be seen again.) Before I had cats I worried about a lot of useless stuff: licking envelopes, cold and flu season, how well other people washed their dishes, etc. When you live with an animal that keeps a box of shit in your house or apartment, then goes directly from that box of shit to your kitchen counter, you tend to forget about the envelope glue and the dishes. You can go head-to-head with the cat, implementing a tactical defense with a squirt gun and aluminum foil, but if the cat *really* wants on the counter, then there's nothing you can do. You can't live your life watching the kitchen counter. Or even live your life applying double-sided tape to the counter—though you can spend a few hours laughing hysterically at the results.

But I admit I never really grasped unconditional love until after I'd had Floyd neutered. I'm rather ambivalent about slowing down the cat population, and so Floyd lived quite a while with his balls intact. He was having a grand time: I'd go walking around the neighborhood and find Floyd five blocks away, nuzzled up to some lady cat. (Of all the bad behavior in my life, I have to say that I've gotten the most grief over my indifference about whether there are more or fewer cats in the world. People have flown into hysterical rages when I tell them that I spay and neuter my cats when I feel like it and not when it would be most beneficial. *But don't you understand how the cat population is out of control? How many are put to death needlessly every year?* I think you could make the same argument for people, but everyone scoffs at that.)

Alas, I decided Floyd's balls had to go after he sprayed my new chair from IKEA. In retrospect, it was kind of a queer chair, and I'm glad I got rid of it at Floyd's unsubtle urging, but I was pissed about it at the time, and so the next morning I took Floyd to the vet. I picked him up that same afternoon: he was groggy, and he opened and closed his mouth noiselessly, as though he were trying to send me a message.

I got the message later that night. I woke with Floyd staring me directly in the face, clawing at the bed.

"Floyd," I said, and pushed his face. "Get the fuck off the bed." I rolled back over and tried to drift off to sleep again.

I didn't get far. Floyd jumped up on the bed and began pawing once more at the comforter. I went to smack his head again, but I missed, and my hand went instead directly into a pile of crap the consistency of a Slushee. As I was barely awake, I withdrew my hand quickly—a natural reaction I suppose—slinging cat crap across two walls, forming a pattern that looked like some horrific postmodern takedown of Jackson Pollock. Floyd had bolted from the room before I'd made it out of the bed, and I was so tired I couldn't even muster the impulse for anger. I took the comforter off the bed, washed my hands with a thoroughness not seen since my crazy days, then wiped down the walls with bleach. Then washed my hands two more times. Then I went back to sleep.

When I woke up the next morning, Floyd was sleeping at the foot of my bed. I considered this. He probably deserved to be punted across the room, and he was in a perfect position for it. But I couldn't bring myself to do it. It may not be the most poignant revelation in human history, but looking at that sleeping cat I thought, *That creature right there that does nothing but cost me money just took a shit*

*in my bed last night; if I'm not going to get upset about
that, then I've got to get over a whole lot of other stuff, too.*

It only now occurs to me that the greatest revelations in
my life are directly connected to the workings of the bowels. I know what that says about my life, but I prefer not to
think about it too much.

Anyway, Lilith had never taken a crap in my bed, and if
I had to choose between being defecated on or screwed
around on, I would take the latter without hesitation. But
the few times Lilith and I saw each other after she'd moved
out, she had a look in her eyes that reminded me of a cat
about to ruin something permanently.

However, Lilith wasn't around as often, and so the tension in my apartment dispersed and gave way to a nonstop
atmosphere of hedonism. My teaching schedule released
me into the world a free man every day by one in the afternoon, and as soon as Cactus, my neighbor, was home from
work, usually around five, I was waiting for him in the
foyer that connected our apartments, beer in hand. A window in the foyer looked out onto the street, and so we sat
there through the evening, smoking and drinking, occasionally one of us rushing into his apartment to pluck
some volume from the bookshelf and accurately recite the
quote that was most appropriate to our conversation.

Julius often saw us from his apartment across the street,
and so he would come and join us, and soon Brenda, who
lived downstairs, would be home and basking in the atten-
tions of a bunch of single and horny men—and yet no one
ever made a pass at Brenda. She was beautiful and genuinely deserving of a good guy, and all of us knew quite
well that we were excluded from that group of gentlemen.

Typically it was Cactus, Julius, and I, but sometimes my friend James would stop by, or Tony, whom I knew because of Cactus, but recently Tony had been showing up at my place as much as anywhere else.

I was having a delightful life, and I had no complaints. I missed my grandfather, but the grief wasn't as heavy upon me as it had been—my dad had found a full-time caregiver to live with my grandmother and take care of her, and so I wasn't having to return frequently to a place that tapped the well of sorrow within me and nearly drowned me in it. And it wasn't solely because of his death—it was tough to be around my grandmother, who was unaware that the love of her life was absent, because in her mind he wasn't absent, and every visit with her was like watching a person drifting farther from the shore, carried into the deep by the undercurrent of time. It was in some ways more terrible than watching a person drown whom you cannot save, because at least the drowning doesn't last for years.

I was only going to Denver on Sunday mornings, and even then I didn't bother to drive the additional three miles from the church to my parents' house. If I saw them at church, either coming or going, that was sufficient. Besides, I enjoyed it when they came to visit my apartment, largely because my mother is allergic to cats.

But life away from teaching was never better: each night I found myself distilled in the company of good neighbors and good drink, and I was beginning to find a pleasure in the Lord's day that I hadn't in at least fifteen years. At the community college I felt like little more than a useless totem of knowledge; sitting in the church with the kids

every Sunday, I at least felt my presence was practical, and
on the really good occasions, moderately helpful.

At some point the idea of teaching wasn't entirely re-
pugnant to me because I felt I'd be helping people find
their way through this world—or possibly confusing them
further, but at least they wouldn't be stuck. Now I felt
stuck, except on that final day of the week when I gathered
with people who were not yet jaded by experience, and
who seemed genuinely interested in how to live life, because it had barely just started for them and everyone else
was afraid to tell them that it wasn't easy, but compared to
the other options it was a pretty good deal.

I was walking out to my car after a not-so-terrible American Lit class on "Rip Van Winkle." Most people have a
memory of some corrupted grade-school version of the
story, either in storybook form or the dreaded filmstrip,
but at least three people in the class demonstrated some
amount of interest in how well Irving's writing stood the
test of time. And also I'd managed to work in an amusing
anecdote about raising a chicken, because it seemed stupid to pay for eggs when you could just keep a chicken
tied up in the backyard.

"You know, I have a chicken."

It was one of my students, a blonde woman of indeterminate age. I was only certain that she was old enough to
drink. I tried to make it out of the class building as quickly
as possible to avoid speaking with students, particularly
females. I'd wised up about that business. If I had to have
them on the brain, best to have them that way when I was

alone with my trusty Vaseline. No need to prove yet again that I was a complete idiot.

It was difficult, however, to ignore her statement. I mean, I was genuinely interested in getting a chicken. If anything, I thought it would be a riot (or a massacre) to watch it interact with the cats. Chickens are fierce, though—a small cat would easily be pecked to death.

"So, why do you have a chicken?"

"Well, it's not really *my* chicken."

"That's even more disturbing. What do you do? Just go around giving other people's chickens away?"

She laughed—she had a fantastic smile. I'd made it a point in class in the past not to notice her fantastic smile. "No, it's where I live, there's this wild chicken . . ."

"Where do you live in Charlotte that there's wild chickens? Is there a refugee village in your backyard?"

"It's at the apartment complex where I live, there's this chicken and no one can catch it. If you want a chicken, you should come catch it."

I would once have mistaken this for a clever come-on, but it was far too bizarre for that. Besides, we'd reached my car and I was ready to make a quick trip back to the house so I could masturbate.

"Well, I doubt I'd fare too well at chicken wrangling. Besides, I don't think a Kia Sephia is designed to haul a chicken, even though it is a Korean car." I indicated my car at my hip.

"Oh," she said, "I'm right next to you. My car is Korean, too."

I looked at her car: a foam green Hyundai. It had a child seat in the back. "You have a kid?"

"Yep. A little boy. He just turned three."

"Far out." But it was not a declaration of surprise. The air had gone out of the conversation for me. I saw the flash of a ring on her finger, and I realized this was just some nutty broad rambling to me about a fucking chicken. "Well, okay. I'll see you later." I didn't even masturbate when I got home; I just went straight for a beer.

I was barely into my second beer when Tony showed up on my back porch. It wasn't yet spring, but you wouldn't know that by the weather—it was seventy degrees and everything was in bloom. Tony had taken off from his sales job early and was sporting a twelve-pack of Newcastle.

"I just talked to Cactus," he said, popping the cap from his beer with his cigarette lighter. "He's knocking off work early and headed home. You got a plate?"

"Yeah, let me go grab one."

"No big deal, your table is clean." Tony dumped a small mound of coke onto my dining table and began to chop it into fine lines. "Man, what a fucking killer day!" He extracted a small straw from his breast pocket and leaned into the blow. Then he offered me the straw.

"You know I only travel in a downward direction."

"I know, but it seems impolite not to at least offer." Tony is Italian; they are a people of manners.

Eventually Cactus showed up—he did like his ups, and so he and Tony fell into a frenetic conversation about oil prices, and whether we were experiencing global warming.

"You know," Tony said, "so like everyone goes to hell, 'cause everyone has done something fucked-up, and babies that die are people who only did a few fucked-up things, so maybe we shouldn't be so sad when a baby dies, do you know what I'm saying?"

"According to Christians we should be glad when one dies, because if a baby has been baptized, then it goes to heaven where it basks in the beatification of Jesus. Ha!"

"What about the unbaptized babies?" I asked.

"They're totally fucked. Jesus is a prick about that shit."

Cactus once told me that his earliest memory is of standing at the screen door of his house, watching a thunderstorm roll in as his mother sat in the hallway, clutching her Bible and praying feverishly for the storm to pass. When he was thirteen, his mother left her Bible open to a particular passage on the front seat of her car and walked into the ocean off the coast of Savannah, Georgia.

Julius walked into the apartment as Cactus was finishing his sentence. He punched Cactus on the shoulder.

"Don't say that shit about Jesus, buddy. That's not nice. Mind if I get one of those beers?"

"Why can't I say what the fuck I want to about Jesus? First of all, he doesn't exist. Secondly, if he does exist, he was just some random dude someone built a good story around that's been popular for an exceptionally long time because of our fear of death. Third, if he does exist and is in fact a divine being, I seriously doubt he would be offended by anything I have to say. He has the knowledge of the universe. What the fuck do I know?"

"Exactly," Julius said. "Is anyone holding any pills?"

I got up and started toward the kitchen. "I've got some."

"Yeah, I've got some, too," Tony said, and produced a large medicine bottle from his pocket. I returned with a dinner plate full of Valium and some random Percocets.

Tony dumped out his stash and began to identify the menagerie of capsules and tablets. I took a few Valium and went to check my e-mail. Like nearly everyone else I knew, I had to obsessively check my e-mail several times a day or I experienced a mild anxiousness that some bit of news that was best digested immediately was slipping past me.

Curiously, there was an e-mail from the chicken chick:

Hey, I know this may seem really random, but I feel like we have a lot in common, and if you don't think it's too weird, maybe we could hang out sometime and get a beer. I'm recently separated, living with my mom and grandmother, so I'm always looking to get out. But here's my number . . .

So she wasn't nutty—she was a frazzled, divorced, single mother living with her own mother. It all made sense now. She was completely desperate and vulnerable. There are few other traits in a woman I find nearly as attractive.

I walked back out into the living room, which was a death chamber of secondhand smoke.

"Does anyone want a bong hit?" I asked. Everyone declined, even Julius, who was usually a reliable toker.

"I'm trying to cut back, man. That stuff's harsh on my lungs," he said, shaking a Parliament into his hand.

I packed up the bong and took a long, leisurely hit—when my brother had gone to Arizona, he'd left me in charge of his bong, a two-and-a-half-foot glass beast. I felt somewhat foolish having it around, as it didn't seem becoming of someone over the age of thirty, but as I could claim to merely be "watching it" for my brother, it at least seemed a temporary foolishness.

"So," I said, "this student of mine just e-mailed me her number."

Tony didn't hesitate. "Well, call her the fuck up and tell her to bring some friends over. You know how long it's been since I've had some young tail? Jesus!" Tony had been married for twenty years; he was constantly lamenting the expanse of time since young tail had last crossed his doorstep.

"I don't think she's so young," I said. "She has a kid."

"Oh, well, definitely tell her to bring some of her friends. Shit. Those single moms are horny broads—are you kidding?"

Julius shook his head. "I don't know, buddy . . . Eh, that's a tough one. Student. Kid." He shook his head again.

"Well, it's not like the student thing is an issue for you." Tony and Julius nodded at Cactus's mastery of the obvious.

"If I call her, we've got to get Brenda up here. We can't make it look like she's walking into a sausage factory."

"Get Brenda to call some of her friends up, too," Tony said. He looked at Cactus. "Who was that one chick she was with that night, the one with the tits?"

"Sandy?" I said.

"Sandy! That's it. Get that Sandy chick over."

"She's married," Cactus said.

"So the fuck am I!" Tony began to laugh hysterically. I picked up my phone and walked out onto the porch.

Patrice said she'd be thirty minutes, but it took her an hour, and in that hour my apartment flowered from a gathering into a certifiable party, with some of Julius's friends floating in along with Brenda and a guy who slept at Brenda's a lot since the beginning of the year, but who she claimed was not her boyfriend. When Patrice finally pulled up, I was standing out at the street so she wouldn't miss the building.

She got out of the car and looked up at my window. "You weren't kidding. I thought that line about people hanging out was just to get me over here."

"And yet you still came."

"I'm a sucker, I guess."

As we were walking up the steps to my apartment, it occurred to me that a lot of illegal substances were just lying about. True, it was rare that I ran into people who were opposed to the substances in question, but I'd made the mistake a few times of whipping out the bong or the pipe with people who believed that one's illegal activities should be confined to the undergraduate years.

It was too late now, though. The music was blaring and Julius's friends had helped themselves to the bong—there was no covering up that smell. And who could guess what snowy remains trailed across the dining table? We walked into a scene of extremely inebriated people divided into several factions, perched over their beverages, all in heated debate about every pointless subject imaginable.

I really wasn't quite sure what to say, so I said, "Can I offer you a tranquilizer, or a beer, or a bong hit?"

"Why, yes," she said. "And yes, and yes."

We spent a long time talking in my kitchen that night, but I don't seem to remember anything we said. I just recall thinking, *Well, this is the one.*

The next day I called Lilith and told her that I thought we were done for good.

"Well, I want my picture back." She'd left a framed picture of herself when she'd moved the rest of her things out; I hung it on the wall when I knew she was coming over, but otherwise I kept it in my closet.

"I'll put it on the porch. You can pick it up after work."

"This isn't over," she said, her voice breaking.

"I'm sorry, Lilith. I think it is. It's for the best."

"Oh, go fuck yourself!" And she hung up.

I was slouched back in a chair, playing the kids in Sunday school "Spanish Castle Magic" from Hendrix's May '69 appearance at the San Diego Sports Arena. I'd begun to play music in the background prior to the beginning of the class, but on this Sunday the song *was* the class. Clocking in at nearly eleven minutes and including a strange guitar solo of mostly chords and with the rhythm section dropping out, the kids were losing patience with Hendrix with several minutes still remaining. They kept trying to ask questions, I kept holding up my hand in a sagelike manner, and they fidgeted while the song played on. I was tempted to subject them to the thirteen-minute "Red House," which was next on the set list, but that wouldn't have left us much time for discussion. I stopped the disc at the end of the song and looked around the room.

"Thank God," Wendy said. "Do you hate us or something? Why did you make us listen to that?"

"Wendy, it's *Hendrix*. Jeez." This from Kip, who aspired

to play the guitar. I had to give him credit. When I was his age, everyone wanted to play like the guy from Dokken. (Not the new guitarist; the second one.)

"Wasn't he on drugs," Sandy announced, rather than asked.

"He was?" It was rare to see Julia so interested.

"Look," I said, "whether or not he was on drugs is irrelevant."

"I don't see how that's irrelevant," Wendy shot back. "Drugs are illegal."

"Yes, drugs are illegal, yes, he was on drugs, but you have to put it in context: it was the sixties in California—everyone was on drugs."

"Like, *groovy man*," Polly said, and flashed the peace sign. I felt mildly embarrassed for her.

"Okay, so here's why I played you that song—"

"Because you wanted to put us to sleep."

"—because we've been having this discussion sort of off and on about how one feels close to God. So, like, what are ways you guys feel close to God?"

Julia yawned audibly and dramatically; everyone stared at her. "Sorry, you guys. I was up late."

"Doing what?" Wendy seemed on the edge of her seat.

"Never mind," I said. "Wendy, how do you feel close to God?"

"I come to church."

"Hm. Any other way?"

"I guess when I pray."

"Okay, but, is there something, like, you know, maybe not so easily associated with God, like something that's maybe kind of like a regular thing you do?"

"Like when I swim," Rich said.

"Yes, exactly! What is it about that?"

"It's like there's not the noise—like I'm alone in my head."

Sandy, who was always quiet and shyly looking at a portion of some piece of furniture, said, "I feel like that when I read."

"Bless you, Sandy. You've just alienated yourself from everyone else in here besides me because you openly admit to reading, but I know what you're talking about."

"I guess I get like that when I play music." Kip appeared to be thinking hard. "It's like . . . another way to pray, but without words? I don't know. I can't explain it."

"No, dude," I said. "That's perfect, and that's what I'm trying to get at here. I mean, you kids know I slink off after this on most Sundays and skip the service. Pastor Jan is a great guy, he's got a way of connecting with people, but the way this church or any church runs the show just *kills me*."

"Are you saying you don't like church?" I couldn't tell if Julia was ready to declare her own disdain for the worship service or for me.

"It's not that simple . . . Okay, but, yes. I'm saying I'm bored with the way church happens. I think the music is lame, I think the whole thing is predictable in a way that I don't find remotely interesting. But there are parts that I completely dig. I like that bit where we take a moment to greet our neighbors, you know? I mean, I personally think we should maybe do a hip-hop-style half-hug-elbow-tap during cold and flu season, but that's just me."

"I'm so with you," Polly said. "I hate touching people's sweaty hands."

"Well, okay. But as I was saying, there are parts that work for me, and I find those things to usually be about the other people, not me. I like that sense of unspoken connection, particularly at the end when we all join hands to pray. Maybe you're praying, maybe you're not. Maybe you're just drawing strength from the fact that you're here, now, in this place with all these other people, and why or why not are questions you're never going to know the answer to, and so it's a type of beauty—do you see what I'm saying?"

Everyone was staring at me blankly, except for Julia, who'd fallen asleep.

Trey Anastasio played the Thomas Wolfe Auditorium in Asheville on March 2, 2001. This was serious business because he was playing a small theater instead of the arenas that he'd played for the previous six years. What was even better was that Milo was coming into town from Syracuse to see the show along with his college roommate Brad. One of my dear friends, Larry, whom I'd grown up with, lived in Asheville at that time, and his wife was out of town. Stars were aligning.

I'd initially thought I wasn't going to make it to the show, but while lamenting this in class one day a student said, "You want tickets? I'll get you tickets." We had class that afternoon before the show, and the guy who'd promised the tickets wasn't there. I'd expected this, but I didn't expect to bump into him on my way out of the building. He handed me a scrap of paper torn from an envelope with a series of numbers scrawled in pencil on it.

"Here's your confirmation number. Tickets are at the window."

I took the scrap of paper from him skeptically. There was no way this guy was on the level.

But he was on the level. Not only did that scrap of paper get me two tickets free of charge, the seats were *exactly* beside Milo and Brad's seats; Milo had purchased their tickets in Syracuse the day they went on sale. It was unbelievable. I never saw that guy in my class again. He got an F for the course.

All of this is simply to explain that it was shaping up to be one of the best days of my life, the translucence right after a storm when the world is buoyant with birth. I had tickets to a show that was anticipated to be of legendary proportions, I was with good friends, I had cash in my pockets, weed, and no worries. I was in arguably one of the great little cities in the country—it wasn't like any other place in North Carolina; the population was quite reasonable.

This was my worship.

The next morning at Larry's, Milo and I sat on the front porch, surveying the mountains, not really talking. Finally I had an actual question:

"Man, I know this might seem random, but last night during the second set my mind was just reeling, and for reasons not really sensical in any way, it came into my head something I'd heard you and Charlie talking about one time, this idea of religion and desire—"

"Theology," Milo corrected.

"—theology and desire. And I had no clue what the fuck you two were talking about then, and I don't now, but at these Dionysian events such as last night . . . I don't know.

I feel like maybe I know what that means? Could you clear this up for me?"

Milo took a pack of Camel Lights from his shirt pocket, shook one out, lit it, and took a deep breath. He sipped his coffee. Then he said:

"Well, at its most simple form: we want God.

"As Freud would say, we're fundamentally complex desiring beings, epistemologically hidden from ourselves, and one way that we can understand ourselves is . . . Well, how about this: we want to know who we are, we want to know our place in the order of things and know the power and comfort and wonder of these realizations, but as we are desiring creatures we exist in a fundamental situation of unknowing.

"The unknowability of God is equated with the unknowability of the self—Freud would specifically say this hidden self is the unconscious—out of which arises powers and potentialities which make up the nexus of attachment and arrangements and contracts we make with the world.

"And because there is this fundamental hidden aspect of our being, the language that best knocks around with our fundamental unknowing is the language of theology, the language which is determined by the very limits of where human knowing stops and the 'something else' starts. Theology is the vocabulary that fucks around in that place, because theology is the language that fucks around with what we can know and what is possible. It's the language that flirts with the impossible, and because we are desiring creatures and therefore determined by the unknown forces of desire, the language of limits, the language of theology, is therefore the vocabulary. You can also make a case very easily that poetry is a theological language, because poetry is a certain vocabulary that trucks with the unspeakable. Theology is the nastier set that includes all vocabulary that deals with limits.

"So what can we say about this? Poetry is a language of desire much as theology, therefore theology is really about the seduction of women." Milo took a sip of his coffee again and looked at the mists rising from the pines that unfurled below us and in every direction. "Man, this is some good fucking coffee. Hey, Larry! Where'd you get this coffee?"

My parents never exerted pressure on me growing up where Sunday school was concerned. I suspect this is because if they had, it would have meant rising two hours earlier than they preferred, and so my brother and I were spared those Sabbath tutorials regarding the Sermon on the Mount.

But the summer I turned fifteen my mother and father determined that what I needed was church-organized social activities, which were manifested in the Youth Group. (*Youth Group*. It practically applies to any group of young people operating in some sort of collective. The Crips are, therefore, technically a Youth Group, as is any high school football team. The Rolling Stones used to be a Youth Group; they are now Active Seniors.)

I was not so enthused about having to attend a Youth Group, especially on Sunday evenings from six until nine. Some quality television shows were aired during that span, and it was also the *summer*. I was supposed to be free from any responsibility whatsoever, save for mowing our impossibly large lawn (technically an abandoned cow pasture).

The guy who ran the Youth Group at the church was something of a celebrity on the local Methodist circuit. He was a fireman down in Charlotte, and he made a long drive every Sunday night to impart hip lessons of the right way of living. Naturally, his hair was slightly shaggy. Naturally, he played the acoustic guitar. *Of course* he punctuated his sermons with contemporary secular music. And then he also played a lot of John Denver. He also had a biblical name: James. Fortunately, he preferred to be called Jim.

My mom escorted me into the church's recreation hall that first night. In terms of the overall embarrassment I've suffered in my life at her hands, this occasion ranks rather low, but at the time I wasn't aware of the full measure of the spectrum, so it seemed a terribly cruel act. All the cool kids came to this Youth Group, even if they went to another church or weren't Methodists. It was the Black and White Ball of Youth Groups.

A volleyball net had been set up in the rec hall, and both sides of the court were jammed with participants. There must have been twelve people playing on each team. The court was parallel to a small performance stage that was two steps higher than the rest of the room, and those steps were draped with all the most lovely girls from the junior high and high school. (If there is a heaven, may I be allowed to walk down the corridor and into the main room of the rec hall once more and see those people as I saw them then: young and beautiful and not yet clothed in the forlorn rags of age. Weren't we all brilliant then? Didn't a light radiate from inside us all that we thought would never go out? I was in a room of angels and I didn't know it at the time, and couldn't know it—how can you ever know the deep joy of the garden except to find yourself outside of it forever and trying to reach back through the thick thorns of years?)

The recreation hall was a box of raucous noise, but as soon as I emerged from the hallway, my mom's hand firmly locked on my arm, the room quieted down and the sounds of INXS briefly swelled from a boom box nearby to blanket the human hush. But my arrival wasn't enough to hold the attention of the room for even a few seconds, and as quickly as everyone had paused to look in my direction, they went back to their business.

Suddenly Jim was in front of me, smiling broadly with his hand outstretched. I gave him a limp handshake and let my mom do the talking. I was sulking. After my mother had related my name and her concerns that I was spending too much time alone in my room, Jim said:

"Well, we're glad you're here."

I stared at the floor. "I don't want to be here." My voice dripped with the glacial indifference of the put-upon teenager.

"Well," Jim said, "there's the door," and he turned around and walked back to the volleyball game. My mom seemed more than pleased with Jim's response.

"Okay then. I'll pick you up at nine." She left me standing there with my hands in my pockets, feeling pretty stupid about what I'd said and how Jim had shut me down.

The weekly program for the Youth Group was organized as part group therapy, part church service. The first half hour was devoted to letting people socialize and shake out all the excess energy that adolescents produce in hormonal abundance. Then thirty to forty-five minutes of sermonizing was delivered in what seems to be the dominate Protestant manner—a mixture of family-friendly stand-up layered with personal anecdotes, woven into a relevant scriptural lesson. This was followed by a brief break for a snack before the remainder of the time was devoted to discussion of what heavy thoughts Jim had just laid down. Although the topics that were mulled over each Sunday evening seemed to vary from one week to the next, they all fell under the blanket lesson of *don't screw up too much and be cool with everyone, even the unpopular schmucks of the world.*

That first night as I sat in one of the forty or so chairs that were arranged in a large circle around Jim, I discovered that the cheerleaders, the football players, the smart and pretty people, and even the dumb, miserably average slobs—they all fretted about the same stupid shit that worried me senseless, and so much of that had to do with fitting in. If these were people concerned with belonging, then these were my kind of people.

The meeting of the Youth Group always concluded in this manner: everyone stood in a circle and crossed his or her arms and then held the hands of the people standing on either side. And then we all said this benediction in unison: *May the Lord bless you and keep you, may the Lord make his face shine upon you and be gracious unto you, may the Lord lift up his countenance upon you and give you peace. Amen.* As I glance back through the looking glass, it seems pretty lame, but maybe it feels that way because it was done without any perspective on the world. I've had some time over the years to seriously think about what it means to call down blessings from God, which is to me an appeal to the sanctity of the universe and the unity of all things. Perhaps what strikes me as lame is the eager earnestness that I recall having then; I wasn't yet a skeptic, but it would ultimately be my experience with the Youth Group that helped make me into one. But that was a few years down the road and I couldn't have seen it coming. I was hooked that first night—and yet I remember few specifics outside of my arrival and departure, mixed with a general sense of being accepted. I walked outside and saw my mom's 1984 Mercury Marquis idling in the parking lot. I hated that car. It was practical. It signified comfort and affordability and—despite its quasi-French name—a complete absence of the concept of beauty. I skulked into the car, silently wishing that my parents would try to put up as good a front as all the other middle-class parents who bluffed with their automobiles that they were more flush than they actually were.

"See," my mom said, "I told you it wouldn't be so bad."

"I didn't have a good time." I looked away from her, out the passenger's window. "So thanks a lot for ruining my Sunday."

"Well, you're coming next week, so get over it."

"Fine. Make me suffer. It's what you do best."

The next week I asked to be taken a half hour early so I could get in on the volleyball.

The Youth Group scheduled a trip to the beach for the last week in July. I rarely had a chance to escape from my parents for extended periods, so I immediately signed up to go along. Besides, when would I ever have a chance to see the true beauties of my school clad in bikinis, and without the aid of a telescope! No, I couldn't pass this trip up.

Jim and his wife and four other volunteer counselors (two women and two men, all in their twenties and in excellent shape) took two vans full of horny Christian teenagers to Myrtle Beach, South Carolina. If the weekly Youth Group meetings (which I hadn't missed since I attended my first one) were the equivalent of group therapy, then the trip to the beach was intensive LSD-based psycho-analysis. Minus any actual LSD, of course, but it might as well have been there considering how my mind was completely blown.

For the whole week we had the mornings and afternoons free to do what we wanted. On some afternoons an excursion to the mall was organized, but most of the day was divided between the beach (which was just across the street from the house the church had rented on our behalf) and the television room of the house. The TV was continually tuned to MTV, and I saw the videos for "Sweet Child o' Mine" and Cheap Trick's "The Flame" so many times that they are permanently seared into my brain. Also Robert Palmer's "Simply Irresistible" and DJ Jazzy Jeff and the Fresh Prince opining about confused parents. I know how difficult all of this is to believe, but there really was a time when MTV showed *nothing but videos*. Those were precious days; we didn't know how good we had it.

At the beach the eyes of every boy and man were tuned to Kitty Norway and Betsy Jennings. Sweet heaven, yes! Those music videos weren't the only images added to the mind's permanent record of visual experiences. Their already well-tanned bodies were draped along the beach as ornaments for the earth. It was too much for me. I tried to hold it together as best I could, but by the third day I was in the bathroom back at the house, firing a load down the toilet in praise to the majesty of God's work. Lord knows, as often as every other guy in that house went to the bathroom, I couldn't have been the only one.

However, it was the nightly youth meetings where Jim's Christian alchemy manifested the real magic, spinning gold out of our ironic, disaffected, leaden teenage souls. Jim didn't raise the roof the first night, but instead slowly pushed us further and further each evening toward the recognition of ourselves in the eyes of the others. Weren't we lonely? Jim knew what it was to be lonely. Didn't we feel the pressure of our friends and family forcing us to put up facades to please them? Jim knew all about that. Hadn't we, at some point, alienated people who didn't deserve it simply because we didn't understand them or wanted to feel better about ourselves? And sometimes, didn't we turn to drugs and sex to make ourselves feel better, and we didn't really feel better, did we? I had no frame of reference for these last two items, but I knew all about loneliness and alienation, and usually when I was lonely, I masturbated and felt much better afterward. I suspected I'd feel loads better after a good romp with a woman, but the drugs . . . no way, man.

By the end of the week everyone was confessing how much he or she loved everyone else. These confessions often happened late at night when we were tired and emotionally drained from Jim's intense programs. I relished these sessions, the most extreme of which occurred when we were divided into small groups of five or six kids plus a counselor and squirreled away in separate parts of the beach house. There was always some artifice to the purpose of the small group, but the ultimate aim was to completely separate you from your ego and make you realize that you were no different from anyone else.

This actually isn't such a bad concept—I've never been on a corporate retreat, but I imagine they pretty much function on the same principle: bonding.

I didn't understand it then, but the church's most basic function is to bind people together in such a way as to ensure harmony within the community.

I'd lost touch with that bond in the last fifteen years, and I was beginning to think that what I needed, and what this Sunday school class needed, was a little bonding. But mainly I was thinking of me—I was still adrift, and if I followed the patterns, I was certain to come across the answers sooner or later.

"Okay, kids. What do you think about a retreat to the beach?"

"For, like, church?" Julia asked.

"Duh, Julia, what else?" Wendy screwed up her face to convey her disbelief at Julia's question.

"Yeah, Julia," I said. "Duh."

I must have been in a righteously good mood when I was possessed to suggest chaperoning a group of teenagers on a spiritual retreat to the beach. My issue about traveling aside (I don't like straying outside of my comfort zone), there was the other, more pressing matter of responsibility.

Of course, I was not really in charge—I was to act as chaperone for the boys since Pamela, the director of Christian Youth Education was a woman, and also to serve as some kind of role model. Patrice was coming along as well—in the last few months she'd become my constant companion, and now she was boldly offering to help shepherd a herd of hormone-crazed, sexually repressed teenagers to a town notorious for drunken deflowerings, the beach of my youth: Myrtle Beach, South Carolina.

The kids were teeming with anticipation for the weeks leading up to the trip. I tried to share their enthusiasm, but the novelty of escaping to the beach and being free from the omnipotent gaze of my parents was a feeling with which I'd become disconnected. I regarded that adolescent exhilaration the way I regarded a cross, with a sense of an elusive nostalgia. I knew what they were all hoping for: a few hours of unchaperoned mania during which they might cop a feel of those forbidden mysteries that swing open the garden gate.

I'd not been to Myrtle Beach in fifteen years, and like everything else that I'd encountered since I'd moved back to the South, I knew that the place we'd be going would not be the place of memory. And yet I suggested this trip because I was searching for the bridge—a pattern of time's wreckage along the coast of people and places long past had slowly been taking shape for years. It was as if everything that was appearing in my life now was a shadow of some earlier life, apparitions of the world before madness and doubt and disaster. I felt closer to myself than I had in a long time, but there were still pieces missing.

The apartment that I lived in was a place that I'd visited several times before I'd left for New York; surely it wasn't just coincidence that I was back there again, and my apartment was a shadow of the last apartment I'd rented in Syracuse—even the streets were similar. And now I found myself shepherding a flock of kids to the beach on a retreat in the same manner as I'd once been guided to the very same beach. Maybe my desire to find meaning in all of this was still just a remnant of my obsessive-compulsive behavior, and yet it felt as though a map was being drawn for me, but every landmark was a riddle that needed solving before I could unearth my own lost treasure: myself.

My concern about the past was simply background to my immediate concerns: I didn't think I would be able to withstand a weekend at the beach tending to teenagers without a place to clear my head.

Fortunately, the Lord works in mysterious ways. As it turned out, the Christian retreat facility was situated right behind Oscar's—a sports bar swathed in televisions. When Patrice and I arrived and saw the bar, it was nearly a transcendent moment for me: what cubit had I added to my life out of anxiety? If I needed a beer to manage my flock, clearly God was willing to cut me some slack on this one.

The events of the evening were such that Patrice and I didn't intersect with the kids from the church until later that night. By then she and I had knocked back a few pints of Guinness at Oscar's, then shared a joint as we walked down to the beach.

When we reached the beach, the sun had already melted into the land behind us, leaving a red ribbon across the ocean's horizon that slowly faded to violet and then a deep blue. Patrice kicked off her shoes and waded into the water until it dampened the hem of her shorts. I've never been one for frolicking in the ocean, especially at night—*Jaws* cured me of that. I sat back on the sand and watched as Patrice walked back and forth in the water, laughing when she was caught by an incoming wave. Down the shore to my right I could make out the faint green lights at the end of the piers that stretched into the water, and I thought about a night some fifteen years before when I'd last walked along the cool, damp sand sandwiched between the bright lights of inessential hotel rooms and the dark currents that could carry you all the way to the beaches of Normandy if you wished it. A thread of my life was knotted at that point in time.

I'd been to this beach on so many occasions, and I felt if I could graph the spaces between visits, I might begin to solve the equation of my existence.

I graduated high school on Saturday, June 1, 1991. The commencement address was given by a local television news reporter, who seemed comfortable speaking with the odd delay/echo of the PA system in the football stadium. It was clear by his delivery that this wasn't his first time giving a commencement address, and I watched him discreetly accept an envelope from the principal afterward and then light a cigarette at the edge of track.

After I'd shed my cap and gown I spent the better part of two hours procuring five cases of Busch Light and two fifths of George Dickel Old No. 8 and then drove with my friend Roger south along Highway 9 all the way to Myrtle Beach.

The week prior to graduation, Jimmy Robinson, a guy who stocked shelves and bagged groceries with me at Galaxy Food Mart, imparted this gem of wisdom: "Man, if you go to Myrtle Beach and don't get laid, then just don't come back. Shameful."

I didn't know if Jimmy was full of shit or on the level. I had a lot riding on the possibility of getting laid, however. I'd only had two sexual partners by then, and I'd yet to have an orgasm with a woman at all. My first two encounters were abysmally mismanaged—I had no clue what I was doing, and I'm not really sure that my partners did either. Or perhaps sex with me was traumatizing to the point that they knew there was no hope for me: I was a bad fucker.

Roger and I had beachfront rooms waiting for us at the Paradise Inn. Since the summer of 1991 it has become a policy of mine to refuse lodgings at a place that advertises itself as Eden-esque. Our rooms resembled the type of cell in which political prisoners are executed with a small-caliber weapon.

I stayed there a single night, woke to a cold, brown shower in the morning, and then took my share of the Busch to the Hampton Inn. Several friends with whom I'd graduated were also staying at the hotel, though only two of them—Jeremy and Larry—were people I'd actually consider friends. Everyone else was what I might describe as first-cousin friends—people who were glad to see you at a party, but they didn't necessarily think to call and tell you it was happening.

We were all out on the beach Monday afternoon, indiscreetly drinking beer that was sweating in a foam cooler.

These were the movers and shakers of my class—Megan, Elizabeth, Tessa, Gary, Kim, Jason T., and Laurie (who had actually graduated the year before but who wasn't one to shy away from a good week of partying). You probably know the same names, the same types—kids who inherited beauty and wealth and the knowledge of proper forks. They usually all played a sport or were on the homecoming committee. Why was I with them? I was the son of people who didn't have indoor plumbing until well into their teens—I was a few steps from being on the right side of the tracks yet. As proof, that afternoon on the beach Megan looked at me and said:

"Kevin, why are you wearing jeans?"

Everyone within earshot paused and looked in my direction; even in the sun's glare I could tell the question had been on their tanned minds—most of these kids lived on the lake; my house was built in a field that had been a cow pasture for the previous century.

I was nonplussed and said, "Hey, don't you watch *Magnum, P.I.?*" I was a huge Magnum fan, and for some reason I thought it was cool how he sometimes wore jeans on the beach, as if to say, *I don't dress for geography; I dress how I feel.*

No one said anything, then I began to laugh, then everyone laughed, and someone said, "Keck, come on. We need another player for volleyball." I leapt up and dusted the sand off my jeans. I was at least blessed with the gift of self-deprecation.

We spent the rest of the day on the beach, our heads hot and heavy from the beer and the sun. At some point I shed my jeans and lay on a towel in my boxers. When I was in high school, I was constantly taking off my pants or whipping out my dick at parties. I was *that guy*. And of course it never got me anywhere because I was afflicted with a terrible compass when it came to finding my way with women. The presence of my dick in the middle of a conversation was greeted with a mix of revulsion and amusement, and oftentimes downright hilarity when I attired it with an onion ring around the head, acting out the mating-ritual bit from the Coneheads on *Saturday Night Live*. But there seemed to be genuine disappointment on the beach that day when my wiener did not emerge to look for its shadow. The facades of proper behavior were on holiday, and half-drunk, half-asleep, I could hear the waves of possibility crashing ever closer.

My second night at the Hampton Inn, Larry and I went down to the vending machine. I've forgotten our exact purpose in descending to the first-floor vending area, but whatever it was, it led to a debate about the selection I'd made. We were standing there going back and forth when two girls walked past, then stopped and stood there staring at us. Larry and I looked back at them.

"Hey," one of them said.

"Hey," I said. Or Larry may have said it. It doesn't matter because one of the girls said:

"What floor you on?"

"Four. You?"

"Three. Room three sixteen."

"We'll remember that. We're four twenty," Larry said.

"You're nearly on top of us already," one of the girls said.

And that was it.

When Larry and I returned to the room the lights were out and there was a lot of giggling and laughter, then the lights would suddenly turn on, girls would scream, and the lights would go back out. Only two girls were in the room: Tessa and Laurie. Tessa was a hard-looking girl who'd been the captain of the softball team. She was trying to work it with every guy in there (except me; I'd already spurned her on the back of a bus during a church youth trip) and no one was having it. When the lights were out, she was thrusting guys' hands into her shirt; I couldn't see, but occasionally I'd hear Gary or Larry go, "Tessa, stop making me touch your titty!"

At one point the lights went on and there on the floor was Laurie with Jeremy's prick out, a can of beer poised over it. Then everyone screamed, the lights were out again, and among the giggles and laughter were the distinct sounds of slurping.

The next night I would hook up with one of the girls from the vending area, a sweet dirty blonde named Elizabeth who was nineteen and from Buffalo, New York. She had a younger sister who had just gotten a pet turtle. She was only the third girl with whom I'd had sex, but the first to talk like the girls in the pornos I'd watched. Oh, the things she said to me those two glorious nights!

Well, not quite. It was really a mess. She had a clue, I didn't, but that time with her is as clear in my mind as if I had woken beside her yesterday, and so where is she now, with those wet words? When she and her friends left at the end of that week to return to Buffalo, she gave me her address and I kept it for years. I never wrote, and in one of those dramatic attempts to break with the past that cause people to throw away love letters and yearbooks, her address got tossed out with a box of other mementos that I felt had outlived their usefulness. I can't count the times my heart has broken over that lost address, and not because I have any romantic notion of *what might have been*, but rather because I want to know *what is*. That brief intersection with Elizabeth from Buffalo fundamentally altered the trajectory of my life. Up until then the whispering voices in my dreams had me ready to bind myself to the mast, but her song of flesh was too sweet and wondrous and I came unlashed. I'm quite certain I did nothing of the sort for her.

Elizabeth and I were going to use the bed in my room our first night together, but Jeremy and Laurie were already frolicking upon it, so we diverted to the shower. But in that sliver of light from the hall that raced across the bed, I saw Laurie's tennis-perfect legs spread beautifully, and I would never see her again.

I am interested in those occasions when we become aware of doors opening, everything sweet and sacred when you finally understand the fragility of each moment, the possibility for tenderness or terror at each click of the second hand, but, dear God, how can you live like that? It's impossible to have that much love for the world, because then you, too, would stand outside the tomb of every heart, weeping consecrated tears but without the power to undo what has been written, and yet it is equally holy to watch the final gate swing heavily upon its hinges, dousing our little patch of desire, steel bolts sliding shut.

I know how it ended for Laurie. It happened just a few

miles from where I'm sitting now, at an intersection I pass
through at least a dozen times a week. It's a common enough
ending: she didn't look because she had the protected left
turn, but her stereo was on and thus she didn't hear the
sirens of the ambulance carrying the heart-attack victim to
the hospital. He was seventy-nine, she was twenty; she died
right there, and his story amazingly kept on going for a
while. But here's the uncommon aspect, the twist no writer
can invent: the ambulance driver was the father of Erin
Monthail, the girl to whom Jeremy had lost his virginity
while Van Morrison's *Moondance* played through on cas-
sette, "flipping over several times" as Jeremy would later
point out. But Laurie could not have known that, could not
have been surprised at the collision of events and metal that
marked her end, and what is similarly strange is the handful
of people who know that peculiar quirk to her story. I doubt
too many of them reflect on it with any regularity, or possibly they don't remember, but I do, and I am unable to fully
explain why I must attest to this and other eccentricities of
fate. Can God worry so meticulously over human matters
and this death that momentarily unites the threads of various
narratives—including my own—so that some design seems
to briefly materialize? Whenever I hear any song from
Moondance, I am flooded with remembrances, only one of
which I witnessed: Erin on her knees in her house, which has
mostly wood-paneled walls because it was built at a time in
the seventies when that look was in vogue, alone with Jeremy
and taking his prideful member in her well-practiced mouth,
the bare moon glowing through the sliding glass doors that
frame their silhouettes; there is the image of the light flashing
on momentarily as Laurie pours beer over Jeremy's erect

cock on the hotel floor, her cry of surprise mixed with laughter and hoots from the spectators on the beds; then there is the surreal scene of an ambulance smashing mercilessly into a small car of indeterminate origin, fragile as the hollow bones of birds.

Sometimes memory is the only act of faith I can manage.

The first night at the beach with the kids from Sunday school concluded with a devotional service. Up until that moment I was fairly certain that maybe the kids might connect with something truly spiritual. I mean, we were at the edge of the fucking Atlantic Ocean.

But then Pamela broke out the crafts. We were in one of the conference rooms of the Christian retreat center. We were arranged in the standard Christian Youth-Group circle, signifying unity and hipness. After a brief reading from Scripture, Pamela started handing out large foam squares to everyone. Puzzle pieces. Then I saw the glitter and glue. I felt my buzz slacken.

The idea was that we should write something creative on the puzzle piece that would inspire other young people at the church to join our merry band of soul searchers. This was not at all what I had in mind when I suggested a spiritual retreat to the beach. Thank God I was at least baked; I could cope with glitter under those conditions. I felt tremendously sorry for the kids; a few of them glanced at me, conveying brief, covert messages of agony.

In all fairness I think Pamela's approach would have worked just fine with kids in middle school. She's an inherently good and decent person. Teenagers need that for sure, but if you want to reach them on their level, you have to be a real fuckup. I wasn't sure how I was going to utilize my talents under these conditions. Particularly since Pamela was playing contemporary Christian music as we glittered and glued.

When the boys and I were finally in our room for the night, spread out on cheap bunks with extrasmall twin mattresses wrapped in urine-stain-proof plastic, it didn't take long for them to register their displeasure.

"Kevin, seriously," Kip said. "What was *that* about?"

The other guys waited for my response.

I shrugged. "Be kind and love one another." Someone threw a sock at my head. "Okay, look. It wasn't what I had in mind either, but we're here, Pamela's in charge, and let's just be nice about it and do our own thing when the time is right."

I went into the bathroom, brushed my teeth, took a Valium and two Benadryl, and went back to my bunk. "Don't stay up too late," I said, and soon I felt darkness wash over me.

Saturday was more of the same. We made little necklaces with wooden crosses on them. I don't recall seeing anyone wearing his or her carpenter's jewelry that weekend.

The kids hit the beach; I admit that since I went bald in my early twenties, intense direct sunlight has lost a great deal of its appeal, so Patrice and I headed south a few miles to the Myrtle Beach Pavilion, where I sought out the famed Williams 1962 World Series pinball bat game. It was a pinball machine that simulated a baseball game, allowing one to "pitch" a ball from the center of the cabinet, then hit it with a flipper shaped like a bat. A series of holes around the playing cabinet were designated "out," "single," "double," etc. Tiny metallic players ran the bases on a small groove in the shape of the baseball diamond.

This was church for me.

Growing up, my parents faithfully ensured that we had an annual family vacation. This yearly sojourn infrequently involved a trip to Disney World, or Monticello, but most often we ended up near Myrtle Beach, and on such occasions my dad and I would spend at least an afternoon visiting one or more of the various arcades along the main strip, spending countless quarters on inning after inning of that baseball game. Alone in my adulthood, when I've stood at the altar of that game, I've been completely saddened by the passing of time; I can feel the ghosts of loss consorting with the phantoms of the future, and I consider if I will ever have a son who seeks out the artifacts of our bonds and thinks of me fondly and is flooded with the absolute love of everyone who has touched this game, and also those who will come after, looking back on him.

By the time we'd drifted out of the arcade and rambled through the mist of pretzel and hot dog aroma and the endless booths hawking funnel cake and the T-shirt shops promising to airbrush *your* Myrtle Beach memories on a thin white cotton T-shirt that could be personalized to your specifications, the sun was low in the sky; the kids would be at supper, and afterward they were promised an hour of go-kart racing at a track adjacent to the retreat center. Patrice and I didn't feel the need to race, and so we took our business to Oscar's for yet another night, easing through a few pints and then a smoky, floating walk down to the shore.

The tide was out, and we found a patch of slick, slightly damp sand that marked the high point of the tide. I leaned back on my elbows, and Patrice put her head on my stomach.

"I wish we could stay here forever," she said.

I didn't say anything. It was a seductive thought. That idea had carried me away from numerous apartments and friendships and lovers. And I was good at it—at least that initial break. But after that, the old sickness of melancholy would predictably take hold, and I'd be agonizing in the still hours of dawn, with red-rimmed eyes and scratching the names of everyone I've loved into my skin and wailing, *Whatif whatif whatif.*

Patrice stood suddenly, slipped out of her shoes, and took off running toward the water. She was wearing a white tank top and a denim miniskirt. This scene had all the elements of disaster built into it: sunset, ocean, intoxicated girl, questionable riptides, recent shark sightings. If anything, I was certain the denim would weigh her down and drown her. I looked up and down the beach—a few evening walkers were straggling along the shore, but it looked as if I was her only chance of survival if she was suddenly in real danger.

And yet I considered that all those fish were using the bathroom in the ocean at any given second. So there you have it: I wasn't completely cured. I still worried about stupid things that would never have bothered me when I was younger. Besides, supermodels were photographed all the time standing in the ocean. Would a supermodel subject herself willingly to fish poo if there was a real threat? I think not. Realizing that, I felt more confident that I would be able to rescue Patrice without hesitation should she need it.

204 Are You There, God? It's Me. Kevin.

She wasn't going to need it, though. She swam as though she were born in the ocean, diving and disappearing until I was driven to the brink of worry, only to shoot up out of the water as a mermaid might, laughing and letting her lean body slice through the water parallel to the shore.

The few people who passed by regarded Patrice with a scowl, as though her absolute abandon offended their sense of proper public behavior. What could be more wondrous than to be walking along the beach at sunset and see a beautiful woman so consumed by her passions that she ran fully clothed into the waters that swayed under the moon's delicate pull?

I'd suspected it the first night she came to my apartment and we stood in my kitchen talking breathlessly, but I knew it as I watched her emerging from the water as a Nereid that I need look no further. Once, when I'd stayed beyond closing at No Borders coffee shop in Syracuse, sharing a bowl with Tela and her boyfriend, Petey, I was bemoaning my perpetual loneliness. When I'd finished, Petey pointed the bowl at me and said, "Keck, someday you're not even going to be thinking about it and a woman is going to walk through the door, and you're going to think, 'Man, she's just hung the moon.' It'll happen when you least expect it, but it'll happen. I know that much." I chalked up what Petey had said to the weed talking. I didn't know what the hell he meant by *hung the moon*. But now I knew, and no other words were capable of accurately framing what I felt: Patrice had hung the moon, and I was going to marry her. When she got to where I was sitting, I stood and clasped her wet body in my arms and sealed her mouth with mine. I was lost in the darkness of closed eyes when the kids from church ran up behind us.

"Go get 'em, Kev!" Kip yelled.

Patrice and I let go of each other with the reluctance of teenagers, and I turned to the group.

"What time is it?"

"Time for you and Patrice to get a room."

The night concluded with more crafts and contemporary Christian music—there might have been some mild group discussion, but Patrice and I were poor support for Pamela; she had to practically beg Patrice and me to "engage more fully" with our craft project. I went to sleep listening to the simple talk of teenagers, and I was sad that one day we would all be dead.

On Sunday morning, after we'd packed everyone's bags in the van and were ready to go, we had a brief prayer service. Pamela made a speech about how everyone had shown his or her dedication to God by coming on this trip. *It's the fucking beach*, I thought to myself.

Then we had a hand-washing ceremony. It was exactly what it sounded like: you washed someone else's hands. A few years ago I would've laid down hard currency for such a treat, but the idea here was to emulate the humility of Jesus as he washed the feet of his disciples. So why weren't we washing feet? Clearly, we lacked serious ambition.

The kids had stayed up late talking; in fact the girls had been allowed to come down to the boys' room because I was there to monitor where everyone's hands were, but as

I've previously mentioned, I was overcome with grief regarding our shared mortality, and so I dove into the safety of dreams. I'd been so deep into sleep that I didn't even hear Patrice come into the room at three in the morning to fetch the girls, lest they come under Pamela's wrath. Hence, they were all on the edge of nodding off as Pamela spoke, but when it came time for the washing of hands, something odd happened.

Álvar Núñez Cabeza de Vaca, who ends up in Texas in 1527 as part of a Spanish expedition, writes about the Native Americans he encountered there. When one paid a visit to another, they often spent the first portion of the visit staring at one another and weeping. Cabeza de Vaca doesn't speculate on the precise emotion, but I like to think that the natives were reacting to the singular beauty of the shared moment, and the recognition of its holiness.

And that was what happened that morning at the beach as we took our turns washing the hands of another: a sudden awareness seemed to settle upon the faces of everyone, and in the quiet of the morning there was the sound of the ocean, the sound of gulls, and all around the sound of each of us washing one another's hands.

Genesis, or The Rest of the Chapters of the Revelation to Kevin

I asked Milo to perform the wedding ceremony for Patrice and me. He'd recently become an Internet-certified minister, and when Milo had the attention of a large group of people, he was quite entertaining to watch. Often Milo exuded what I would consider a true *melancholia*—he was of good humor, but it was the humor of a man cheerily playing the piano to an audience of one on the deck of the *Titanic*. He treated crowds as congregations, and his wonderful Southern hipster hospitality and irreverence would take over. After Charlie died, Milo seemed to lose interest in a career in academia and moved back to his old stomping grounds, Elon, North Carolina, and had promptly sold his soul to the banks for a restaurant and a bar. He was doing what he did best: guiding people into intoxicated states of being, whether by the alchemy of his skillet or the straightforwardness of his taps.

Patrice and I were married at the beach, at a house owned by my uncle John. It had the benefit of not only being free, but also my family was gathering there for Thanksgiving, so it made everything that much easier. The friends we wanted to join us would be more than likely vacationing from work, and thus their presence would be ensured. I had a negative bank account balance the day of my wedding, and a tremendous student loan debt. I had no savings, and I owned so few possessions that I could easily name them all. Quite simply, Patrice would soon discover that my life was a sham. My God, I was a single man who lived with seven cats in a two-bedroom apartment! I had some serious soul-searching to do, and sooner rather than later, but this chick was *marrying me*—what the fuck was *her* problem? And furthermore she trusted me to help raise her child? I couldn't return a video on time, and I lived *two blocks* (and these are Charlotte city blocks, which are about a third of the size of a New York City block) from the video store, and I went past that video store *every day*, *twice a day*, and I still incurred fines. If I couldn't be trusted to lift an eight-ounce plastic rectangle from the coffee table and just hold on to it for five minutes to avoid paying money (which I didn't have), how the fuck could I be trusted with someone's kid?

At least he could already talk. That way he could tell me when I was fucking up.

One morning while his mother was working, Gavyn and I had gone to Wal-Mart after a hefty helping of oatmeal and eggs. I was feeling slightly bloated by the time we hit the toy aisle, and enough other people were in the vicinity that I thought I could discreetly release some flatulence and just about anyone could be blamed.

It was—how to say this politely?—*of a sturdier brand* than what I thought was in the cask.

Gavyn had his attention on the Transformers in front of him.

"Hey, Gavyn, let's go look at the Matchbox cars on the next aisle."

"Okay," he said, and I took his hand and pulled him toward the end of the aisle; he wouldn't budge.

"Wait!" he screamed.

"What? What is it?"

He cocked his head and said quite curiously, "What's that smell?"

I felt my face begin to go red and I laughed nervously. "I don't smell anything."

"What's that *smell*? It's bad."

I was yanking on his arm, but he stayed fixed in place.

"It smells like . . ." He paused to consider his options.

"You're probably smelling the detergent on the other aisle." I was literally dragging him now.

"No, that's not detergent. It smells like poop."

"I don't smell it." I could hear the snickers of children and adults behind us, but I knew they wouldn't be laughing for long.

So this was what I was getting myself into: a legally binding contract and a tiny being who felt the need to publicly announce the presence of flatus. My life wasn't supposed to turn out like this at all, no, not this at all.

And it wasn't turning out like that: a curious snag had developed, one that I feel I couldn't have invented had I tried. North Carolina is a strict state when it comes to divorce—the powers that be take marriage vows quite seriously (it is a sacrament, after all), and a couple has to be separated for an entire year before a divorce can be granted. I suppose the legislators who put that law on the books were hopeful fellows, believers that time heals all

210 Are You There, God? It's Me. Kevin.

wounds. From what I've witnessed in North Carolina, after a year of being forced to remain married to someone
you hate, a lot of divorces become nastier affairs than
they might have been had the parties been able to extract
themselves from the arrangement in a more expedient
manner.

Patrice and her husband had been separated for well
over a year, but as soon as he received the divorce papers,
he went into a coma. Seriously.

Granted, he had cancer, and he was undergoing aggres-
sive chemotherapy, but what timing! (Also, it did cross my
mind that I was marrying a woman who was divorcing a
guy with cancer—that's pretty hard-core. Some might even
say heartless. But after Lilith, my gauge on ice queens was a
bit skewed, so I was probably less concerned than other men
might be.) If he'd wanted to find a completely new way to
remain a thorn in her side, he'd done it. The scenario was so
ridiculous I couldn't even get upset. He came out of the
coma within a few days, but he was in no hurry to sign the
papers. I suppose I can't blame him. Impending death and
an actual coma might possess me to approach paperwork
with a bit of indifference. However, the lag in the divorce
papers going through the mail and the judicial system meant
we couldn't legally be married until after December 9. The
invitations were out, and we'd rented an additional house in
which to have the reception, or as Patrice and I called it, the
absolute throw down of 2005. There was no way we could
postpone the wedding. We'd have to fake it.

You can stand in front of a church full of people and God
and make promises to your partner all you want, but it doesn't
mean squat unless you pay the state what is essentially a

veiled bribe so that they'll issue you a piece of paper saying you're married. It's absurd. The state's only interest in marriage is in keeping track of who is where and with whom so that they can send tax documents to the proper address.

So on the appointed day we gathered at the gazebo and recited our vows for the sole benefit of our relatives—everyone else knew that this was pure theater. To my knowledge not a single member of the wedding party was remotely sober— J. R. was wearing a fucking kilt of all things and actually gave a somewhat involved lecture on the historical purpose of his kilt pattern while we were waiting for the festivities to commence. During the ceremony it was all too obvious that Milo was thoroughly shit-housed. If it wasn't a tell that he performed the entire ceremony in sunglasses, then his twenty-minute rambling from the book of Isaiah concerning God's love of witnesses should have been a dead giveaway. And if not, his general pronouncement that love was for renegades and otherwise a doomed enterprise in today's world should have clued in the family and other wedding guests that Milo was preaching in a shamanistic tradition.

But ultimately Milo wound down his performance, and Patrice and I exited to Ben Folds's cover of the Cure's "In Between Days." When you've found someone who will allow that to be the concluding song of your marriage ceremony, you know you've found the right person.

Because the wedding had been a masterful ruse, and because we didn't have time for a honeymoon since I had to return to my teaching duties pretty much immediately, life didn't change that much except that I was wearing jewelry for the first time in my life. Patrice, Gavyn, and I were still wedged into the apartment with the seven cats, and nearly every night Cactus or Julius stopped by for a beer. The most meaningful change was that we took our smoking to the porch. As Gavyn was a full-time resident lacking the capacity for reasoning that secondhand smoke was a death sentence, we decided for him that he should only be subjected to toxic levels of cat dander.

As far as I was concerned, it was great being married, because I actually wasn't.

Or what I mean is that my marriage was only as good as my word, because that was about as much legal claim as Patrice had upon me. It was fantastic being married without any of the actual consequences of such a monumental commitment—I was free to back out of the deal at any time, and the only thing that would be unpleasant would be the explanation to my family. And also the return of certain gifts—I'd always wanted a deep fryer. I couldn't go back to baked fries—they just didn't taste the same.

I was in the kitchen shortly after the turn of the New Year, just six weeks after our wedding pageant, frying up some seasoned curly fries when Patrice burst in from the living room, screaming:

"God, what are you cooking? Are you trying to make me puke?" It was January, but she opened every window in the apartment, cranked the heat, and threw my basket of fries off the back steps and into the wilted garden below.

I could have asked her what the fuck her problem was, but I'd recently been working on that part of marriage where one keeps quiet in a tense situation.

I had not, however, learned to avert my eyes from other

women, and that caused an issue later that night when we went for a drink at Jackalope's with Cactus. I'd like to blame it on Cactus, because he pointed out the girls in the first place, but we were on our fourth round by then, and it took me a while to focus and let what I was seeing settle in: two marginally attractive women kissing. An odd occurrence for that bar, so it was certainly noteworthy, but I wasn't especially moved by the occasion, and so I had Cactus continue to explain to Patrice why astrology was just a deception created by vague language, and that to believe otherwise is just to indulge a basic human urge to read patterns into random noise.

"I mean, it's all a matter of probability, Patrice. People tend to attribute great stock to when you guess correctly, and they forget the times you're incorrect. You see—"

Patrice grabbed her purse from the table and headed for the women's restroom.

"Man, she takes that stuff a little too seriously, don't you think?"

"I don't know what's up, Cactus. She threw my french fries out this afternoon because she hated the smell."

"Steak fries?"

"Curly."

"Mm. That sucks."

On the way home, as we turned the corner from Seventh onto Clement, she said, "So did you like looking at those fucking whores?"

"What whores?" I turned around and scanned the street; I honestly had no idea what she was talking about.

"You know what whores. Back at the bar. Those bitches kissing. I saw you take a good long look."

"Patrice, I'm kind of wasted here. I could barely focus." I was more cooked than Patrice realized. I'd gone to the dentist a few days prior with a miserable toothache, and I'd had yet another wisdom tooth (this one from my lower jaw) yanked out. I'd not used my usual dentist, who was frugal with pain medication, but instead chose an oral surgeon who was guaranteed to hook me up with a bottle of Vicodin.

"Bullshit, motherfucker." Patrice stormed off to the apartment. When I got home, I found one of the panes of glass on the back-porch door smashed out—she didn't have a key with her, and she wasn't waiting for me. I was glad Gavyn was staying at his grandmother's; there was no telling how this was shaking down.

When I walked in the living room, she was dead asleep on the couch, an empty snack-cake wrapper still clutched in her hand.

The next morning she walked into the kitchen as I was making coffee and said, "I think I need to get a pregnancy test."

I scooped the Folgers into the filter and turned the coffeemaker on.

"Well?" she said.

"Well, I guess I'm going to take a Vicodin. You going to get the test now?"

Thirty minutes later my Vicodin had kicked in and Patrice was holding the pregnancy test in her hand.

"So what are we looking for?"

Patrice was biting her lower lip. She stood up from the bed and picked the packaging out of the garbage. "One blue line means no; two means yes." She sat back down on the bed. "You ready?"

"Wait—what do you want to happen here?"

"I don't know," she said. "What do you want?"

"I don't know either. Just fucking reveal it."

Patrice pulled back her hand and started to laugh and cry simultaneously. I examined the stick, then lay back on the bed.

"Fuck," I said. "I guess we're going to have to actually get married now."

This little surprise presented some problems, most of which were financial. It was also surprising to me because I'd (foolishly, kids, foolishly) been having sex with women for years without any protection whatsoever, and I'd long ago assumed I was sterile. I mean, I'd been flooding vaginas with millions of sperm at a clip, and in sixteen years the closest I'd come to inseminating someone was a late-period scare with my undergraduate girlfriend. Plus you hear all that stuff about marijuana lowering sperm count. Lies, children, all lies.

It was costing us at least a grand a month just to keep a roof over our heads and the utilities connected. With one more child in the mix, plus the associated costs of diapers, formula, health care, etc., things were looking bleak. Patrice picked up some cash every now and again by utilizing her cosmetology license—she's quite brilliant at styling and coloring hair—but even if she launched into it full-time as she had done before meeting me, and with the community college essentially using me as exploited labor, our level of comfort was about to plummet. *Sacrifice?* The word was becoming more familiar to me every day.

Plus I had no place to stash another person in my apartment, and I wasn't really ready to leave. It had taken me several years of bouncing around the Charlotte area before I'd at long last found a place that was a beautiful coalescing of all those elements for which I was perpetually searching. I began working out plans to convert the dining room into a nursery. I'd wanted to repaint it anyway, because Lilith had picked out its current magenta color.

"What are we going to do about the cats?" Patrice asked one night as we were sitting on the couch watching an episode of *Law & Order*.

"What about the cats?" I looked around the apartment. It was impossible to cast your gaze in a direction where there wasn't a cat.

"We can't have a newborn in a house full of cats."

"Why not?" I was genuinely bewildered about this.

"Because they're not clean! They have shitty little feet that go traipsing their shitty little germs all over the place! Do you know how often I wipe down the sink in the bathroom because there are paw prints in it?"

"It's a fucking sink."

"And I like my sink to be free of shitty little cat germs. Is that so wrong? Is that too much to ask? Besides, I'm pregnant—pregnant women shouldn't be around cats to begin with."

"I thought that was an old wives' tale."

"No, they have a bacteria in their shit that can kill a fetus."

It all made sense. "They truly are the master species. They enslave us by making us work at jobs we hate so we can feed them, then when we come home depressed, we turn to them for comfort, and they put their turds in a box, which we willingly shovel out like we're searching for gold. And they can kill us silently, in the womb. I'm truly in awe of these little beasts. Let's name the kid after one of the cats."

Patrice got up off the couch, walked to the bedroom, and shut the door with restrained authority. Deaf Cat hopped up on the couch next to me and put his front paws on my shoulder. I scratched behind his ears. "I don't know, Deaf Cat. It doesn't look good for you guys." I turned and looked at him. "Why the fuck am I talking to you? You can't hear a word I'm saying."

When I told my parents the news about Patrice's pregnancy, they didn't seem stricken with panic as they'd been in the past when I made major life-changing announcements. I didn't know what to make of this except that they figured I was married now, and thus I was essentially someone else's problem. Finally they could just sit back and enjoy the impending disaster without feeling obligated to help pick up the pieces.

My dad was still a practical man, however. "So where are you moving? You can't stay in that apartment. Not with all those cats."

"Can everyone just lay off the cats?"

"You've got too many. It's weird."

I didn't respond to this.

"Look," he said. "You all need to be saving money. The house—"

"Absolutely not. We'll move into a crack house first."

"It's just sitting there, Kevin. It's even furnished."

"Can't do it, man. It's just . . ."

"Yeah, I know."

In October, about six weeks prior to the wedding, my dad, in his role as administrator of my grandmother's estate and general well-being, concluded that it was time to move her to a place where she could have around-the-clock care from medical professionals. It was clearly the logical thing to do: she rarely recognized any of her children, she was barely mobile without assistance, and it was simply too much for one person to look after her.

My grandfather had been adamant that my grandmother would go to a nursing home only over his dead body. Well, true enough. I can't suppose to know what heavy labors of the heart my dad toiled under to make that decision.

My grandparents' ex-house had become a warehouse for the evidence of their existence: clues and questions, but the answers lie buried in the earth and the infertile soil of my grandmother's mind. My dad was ready to chase out the ghosts—he'd already begun to repaint the walls and put down hardwood floors, but I wasn't the man to bring the cleansing voodoo.

"I'm probably going to rent it out if you don't want to move in . . ."

"Rent it out," I said. "How often do you get to feel like a feudal lord?"

Patrice's belly started to swell almost immediately after we discovered she was pregnant. This didn't set off any alarms with me. What did I know about pregnancy? But Patrice had been through this routine before, and she seemed distressed.

"I think this happened on our wedding night."

"How do you know that?" I was actually thinking, *Oh, fuck. This baby is going to be a village idiot.* I knew exactly what chemicals had been fertilizing Patrice's brain and liver; this egg was saturated in Valium, opiates, and alcohol.

"Look at this." Patrice was standing in profile, her shirt pulled up and her pants down slightly. "Look at how big I am already. I'm at least twelve weeks."

I did the conversion in my head. "Three months?"

"Yep."

"Man. Should we start planning or something?"

After six years I considered myself relatively cured of my fear of death by germs. Plus, any lingering compulsions I had went right out the window the first time I had to wipe my grandmother's ass. However, I was still not keen on hanging out in hospitals or doctors' offices. I believe in my immune system and the power of soap, but I also know that medical facilities are where superviruses get their start.

But medical offices and hospitals were becoming frequent

stops on my itinerary. Patrice had told me even before we were fake-married that her first husband hadn't really made it to all the doctor's appointments when she was pregnant with Gavyn, and I was determined to outdo him on at least that level. Patrice had hesitated a second too long when I pressed on whether my penis was larger than her first husband's—she ultimately assured me that it was, but I just didn't buy it. If I wasn't valedictorian, I was at least going to have perfect attendance.

Usually I was extremely tense during these visits because I was trying to touch as few surfaces as possible, but I was nearly giddy on the ides of March, which was also our first ultrasound appointment. Patrice and I were both the type of children to clandestinely peel back the wrapping paper on our Christmas gifts several days beforehand because we couldn't stand the anticipation. Thus, we weren't going to be surprised in the delivery room either. Besides, knowing the gender would fill the gift registry with much more informed selections.

We were in a darkened room; Patrice was on the exam table, the small hill of her belly lubed up with some ruefully sticky gel designed to help the sensor get a more accurate picture. Or something like that. I wasn't really paying attention to what the nurse was saying.

I was watching a monitor, and it looked just like static, and then this tiny peanut with arms and legs appeared on the screen. It actually looked quite like Mr. Peanut, minus the top hat and cane. Especially the cane.

"Looks like you're going to have a little girl."

Patrice burst into tears yet again. If she wasn't throwing

up, she was crying, and if neither of those were happening, then it was eating or sleeping. So far this pregnancy thing was kind of a drag. Sure, I was participating in the creation of life, but untold billions of people had already proven it could be done.

The dark room was making me sleepy. I wished I were stoned; the peanut would probably look a lot cooler then.

"I'm going to be right back," the nurse said suddenly. "I'm looking at your labs here . . . probably nothing . . . but I may need you to have some more blood taken before you leave." She moved quickly out of the room.

Patrice reached out for my hand. "What do you think it is?"

"Like she said, it's probably nothing. If Cactus were here, he'd tell us that statistically the simplest explanation is the most common one. *Nothing* seems pretty simple and common."

The nurse stepped back in as I finished speaking, and she glided into her chair, grabbed the ultrasound wand, and whisked it over Patrice's belly, saying, "Ah, ah," as she did so.

"What? What is it?" Patrice said.

"Well, here's the heartbeat," the nurse said, working the wand with one hand and her computer keyboard with the other. An EKG reading raced across the screen, and the *wah-wah* swish and thud of a newly formed heart sounded in the room. "And," she continued, moving the wand, "here's the other heartbeat." A second EKG readout appeared below the first.

Patrice's voice quivered. "You mean my heartbeat."

The nurse laughed. "No, not yours. You're having twins, and it appears as though . . ." She worked the wand around, and two white peanuts floated on the screen. "It looks like they're identical. Two girls."

Patrice looked at me and erupted into tears, but she was smiling.

I felt the blood go out of my face. I remembered immediately my ranting appeal to the abyss: *a little bonus, like a hot set of twins or something . . .* My wife is a former Teen Miss South Carolina. There's no doubt they'll be hot, and in one stroke of vexing fate a man's greatest fantasy becomes my worst nightmare. Cactus would say, *Well, clearly, Keck, in an infinite universe it's more than probable that out of all the things you might "pray" for, some of them will actually come to pass. What about all the ones that don't? And you know what? That would be the more amazing thing: to live in a universe without coincidence.*

"Kevin. Kevin!" Patrice had reached out and was gripping my arm.

"What?"

"Are you okay?"

"Me? Yeah, I'm fine. I'm just curious to see how all of this unfolds."

I could probably have said something more nurturing and romantic, but I was genuinely in shock. I like to think my life is a series of average moments that occasionally gather enough steam to turn up a surprise, but I couldn't have been more stunned had I woken marinated in menstrual blood, hanging from a meat hook in a lion's cage while being sodomized by a penguin with a flute. Fifty years ago a decent doctor would have had a bottle of brandy on hand to bring my color back.

The twins were due in late August, but by mid-June Patrice was thoroughly miserable; she looked like an egg perched on toothpicks. I was also suffering—listening to Patrice complain about her situation was driving me bananas. I never voiced this to her, though. What were my daily labors compared with having two creatures growing inside her? Besides, I rarely had time to reflect on what was going on around me—since we'd discovered we were having two babies instead of one, everything had hit the fan. We moved out of the apartment within a week of our first ultrasound appointment and into the house that had belonged to my grandparents. It was not easy to suddenly sleep and fuck just three feet from where my grandfather had drawn his last breath, so I spent many sleepless nights with my head pressed against Patrice's stomach, listening for the whale song of the womb, and looking across the smooth dune of her belly to the line of trees and the darkness looming outside.

Thus, when I wasn't working, I was readying the house for the imminent arrival of babies and attempting to sweep out all the old specters. And attempting to keep my mother's madness on the other side of the door. The scene was essentially still the same; the lawn mower was still sitting in the basement awaiting its phantom internist. I wasn't going to get around to it anytime soon. In eighteen months I'd gone from a bachelor to a married father of one, and that was soon to blossom into three. How did that happen? It only seems a few pages ago that I was still in Lilith's clutches, and suddenly my life was more of an abstract than the fleeting sweetness of the sound and fury of a mad, rambling epic. I'd spent five years away in Syracuse, and I'd been back five, and so much of that time I'd felt totally adrift and doubtful that I would ever find any peace. But here I was again on the shores of my beginnings, and this time my return felt right. The course was mysterious. Charlie's mantra helped to dispel the darkness: *A cow is just a cow. It doesn't know it's a cow, it's not concerned with being a cow, and you've got to be a cow, motherfucker!*

I needed to have questions answered so badly at one time in my life that I was positively tragic. Oh, the calamity of it all! Poor me! I'd built a castle of false hope on the shifting sands of chemical enhancement, and I'd found solace where I least expected it: in cleaning my grandmother's ass and in the company of kids who were just beginning to grapple with the essential ambiguities of existence.

My faux marriage became a real marriage across the street from the Sidetrack Grill, in Elon, North Carolina, the day after Patrice and I went to a concert in Raleigh in late June; the kids I'd tried to mentor had to learn the most harsh reality about mentors: they disappear, often with little or no warning. The days of sweet intoxication faded into a sober shouldering of responsibility. The twins were delivered by emergency C-section a month early.

It felt just like that: I'm married, I'm not teaching Sunday school, babies—*bam! bam! bam!*—the click of Buffalo Bill's revolver putting holes in those years.

A nurse was at the door of the room where I waited in hospital scrubs, beckoning me to follow her: she smacked a large silver disc on the wall and the doors to the operating room swung open.

As I was seated beside my wife, the doctors and nurses quickly got down to business, and every wrong turn I'd made suddenly seemed irrelevant. I wanted to retain each detail: the book I was reading just moments ago in the waiting room: *Michael Martone* by Michael Martone, a curious title to have on hand for the birth of twins; the double doors into the operating room; the doubled staff; the anesthesiologist, Hans, who narrated with his German accent what was happening, joyfully reassuring Patrice and me that everything was going perfectly—it was possible that my grandfather and Hans's grandfather had been conscripted to try to murder each other by the madness of conflicting bureaucratic ideologies, and now we'd been woven into this same moment by a phantom chicken and chance and the incalculable decisions and revisions of governments and managed health care, and it struck me as completely fucking odd that any universe would go through all that trouble to play the most fantastic prank on me I could ever have imagined.

I held my wife's hand.

Perhaps the divine is always speaking to us in the language of coincidence, and we call it as such because we can't understand the greater design. I recall quite vividly the sensation when the first baby was yanked into being— I was witnessing the world for someone else, and for the first time I felt as though I was where I was supposed to be, and I wasn't worried about myself at all.

Vanity of vanities! All is vanity . . .
There is no remembrance of former things, nor will there
be any remembrance of later things yet to happen among
those who come after.

—*Ecclesiastes*

Acknowledgments

I suppose I should offer some words of gratitude to the people who've helped me along the way:

My teachers in Charlotte: Sarah Welch, Robin Hemley, Chris Davis, and Fred Smith made me believe I could string some words together in a pleasing fashion.

When I made it to Syracuse, Michael Martone taught me a very essential lesson about being true to your work and above all doing the right thing.

And Charlie Winquist? Here's a story: One time he was on his way to meet a woman for a drink, and in his eagerness to make it to the bar on time he crossed the street without looking and was hit by a bus. He got up, dusted himself off, and walked into the bar. When he met the woman she commented that he looked a little ruffled, and he said, "Yeah, I just got hit by a bus." She insisted on taking him to the hospital, and it turned out he had some internal injuries that warranted a stay overnight for observation. Charlie said, "Well, can I smoke?" The doctor told him of course not. "Then I'm going home," and Charlie got up to leave. "Okay," the doctor said, "I've got this guy who just had heart surgery . . . he insisted on smoking too. You can share a room with him." Charlie would later remark: "A lovely fellow. You couldn't have wished for a better roommate under the circumstances." And the lesson? It's a short life. Meet it upon your terms, but never keep a woman waiting, even if you've been hit by a bus.

Chad Snyder has insisted that he will only accept an acknowledgment if his name appears on a separate line from everyone else's.

Jack Lawrence did not make such a request.

John Whitley: *vox clamantis in deserto*.

To my brother, Brandon: you've never once told me you love me when you're sober, you schmuck.

If the devil ever comes for my soul, he only gets 85 percent—the rest belongs to my agent, Erin Hosier, who is shrewd and beautiful. I mean, she has to be to have sold a book like this.

And last but not least, my editor, Lindsay Sagnette, the exquisite angel who descended to earth to breathe life into my words.

Also, to Jeff Parker: it's never the same without you.

A Note on the Author

Kevin Keck is the author of *Oedipus Wrecked*, a collection of essays, and a frequent contributor to Nerve.com. His writing has appeared in *Maxim* UK, *Details*, and numerous dust-collecting literary journals. He lives just outside Charlotte, North Carolina.